R 1, 99

),

986

MW01017123

FIRE FROM THE SKY

A DIARY OVER JAPAN

By

Ron Greer and Mike Wicks

Copyright © 2005 Ron Greer; Mike Wicks

All rights reserved. No part of this publication may be reproduced, transmitted in any form or by any means electronic, mechanical, photocopying, recording or otherwise, or stored in a retrieval system without the prior written consent of the publisher. Reviewers may quote brief passages in connection with a review written for inclusion in a magazine, newspaper or broadcast.

First published in 2005

Hardcover ISBN 0-9768712-0-3

Inquiries regarding purchasing copies, or requests to reprint all or part of Fire From The Sky: A Diary Over Japan should be addressed to Ron Greer at the address below.

Ron Greer
205 Harris Road
Jacksonville, AR
72076-3603

Tel: 501-982-3626
E: diaryoverjapan@aol.com

The authors, publishers and all others directly or indirectly involved with this book assume no responsibility or liability, direct or indirect, to any party for any loss or damage by errors or omissions regardless of cause, as a consequence of using this book, nor accept any contractual, or other form of liability, for such use.

Cover Design and Book Layout by Tom Spetter; Cyan Design (www.cyandesign.ca)
Editorial Services provided by Sharon Ellinghausen
Printed and bound by Friesens of Altona, Canada

WORLD WAR II
"AIR CREWS"
DEDICATION

Yet from those of our number who fly no more, we must accept a trust - the trust of men who gave their lives in order that there may be a free life for others - and should we, in the future, treat lightly the foundations of that free life, we will have betrayed these men to whom, for all time, must we be indebted.

As the radio operator on the B-29 Superfortress 'City of Monroe', Staff Sergeant Herb Greer would, in 24 long and gruelling combat missions, explore the full spectrum of human emotions. From the initial jitters of expectation facing the unknown, to stark terror as the world around him exploded in brutal violence that is the heartbeat of combat, to professional satisfaction in completing the mission successfully, Herb would feel it all.

Nels Running, Major General, USAF (Ret)
Executive Director of America's
Commemoration of the Korean War 2000 - 2003

"SON'S DEDICATION"

I have merely presented here in book fashion, that which had already been recorded, first and foremost in a "diary" written over Japan, while in harm's way. Secondly, in the minds of those living legends, who made up the crew of "the City of Monroe" B-29 Superfortress, who for all intents and purposes conceived this book through their unselfish efforts, wanting not just to preserve their own liberty and freedom, but that of mine, yours and all Americans. It is my wish and hope that we continue to share this time in history, not only with our current generation, but moreover, with all subsequent generations. All Americans—your family, my family and subsequent families ongoing— have a role to play in our history, because as Americans if we don't carry this message, we will have surely failed, not only ourselves, but those individuals who were willing to accept the risks necessary, to make possible that which we sometimes take for granted; "Our Freedom" paid for in full, by that Great Generation.

Your Proud and Loving Son, Ron
I dedicate this book to my hero...............my father..............my friend!

S/MSGT Herbert L. Greer, USAF Retired

TABLE OF CONTENTS

ACKNOWLEDGEMENTS

I would like to convey my deepest thanks and appreciation to the following individuals whose efforts and support made this book possible:

To Susan Rea whose initial involvement created the spark to pursue this endeavor.

To Dawn Townsend whose persistent encouragement helped me through the frequent roller-coaster like emotional rides of researching, writing, rewriting, etc.

To Judy VanNewkirk whose expertise and creative enthusiasm enabled me to develop a marketable product with which to begin my search of a co-author.

To Pete Weiler of the 39th Bomb Group website and SallyAnn whose work on B-29's Then and Now, through her 56 years ago web site provided much needed information.

To Michael Wicks the co-author. His writer's "rainmaking" expertise and experience has made all this possible. Through his endeavors we were able to convey not just historical information as it was, but place you there some 60 years ago.

To Ingrid Vaughan for her assistance with the chapter 'Queen of the Skies'.

To Tom Spetter for his design excellence of the cover and layout of the book.

To the editor Sharon Ellinghausen for her support and contributions.

To Ken Stratford for coming up with such an evocative title.

Ron Greer

FOREWORD

I'm in Arkansas sitting with World War II veteran Herb Greer and his son, on their patio in Jacksonville.

Herb is 83 years old and wearing a baseball cap with a B-29 bomber embroidered on it with the words 'City of Monroe' written above, less we confuse it with any lesser aircraft. Encircling the hat there are a plethora of pins depicting medals and allegiances to associations, both old and new.

He is smoking heavily, a habit he tells me he picked up in order to while away the long lonely and frightening hours as a radio man 60 years ago during the firebombing of Japan in 1945.

A few months previously, out of the blue Ron Greer, Herb's son, called me and asked whether I would be interested in bringing life to a book in progress that he and his father had started writing. They had contacted several publishers and along the way my name had come up. They had spent the previous three years assembling information about the Pacific War and more particularly the role the B-29 and its crews had played in bringing Japan to its knees during the latter part of the war, some weeks after Europe was celebrating victory.

Now, in the early Spring of 2004, Ron and Herb are showing me hundreds of photographs. Photographs of bombing raids on Japan. I see bombs falling from the bellies of groups of huge bombers, I see them hitting their targets, innocent small puffs when photographed from several thousand feet - on the ground it was a different matter.

I look over at Ron and can tell that he is devoted to his father, but that's not all, there is hero worship here. Ron is immensely proud of his Dad and the role he played in the war and wants to see his story told.

But, this book is not an ego piece it is for all the young men who went to fight for freedom – those that lost their lives and those that survived, but lost their youth. 'Freedom isn't Free' is a mantra repeated at the Greer residence.

I turn back to the photographs, there are many of B-29 bombers; three in a group flying past Mount Fuji, dozens flying cheek to jowl dropping hundreds of bombs which look as if they are only just missing their fellow flyers' ships by inches, a photograph from a war time magazine shows a Japanese officer beheading a captured airman.

I was born after Herb's war was finished, but although Ron is a contemporary of mine he has made it his business to know. He has spent years sitting on this patio talking with his father about his wartime exploits, taping their conversations and stories, gathering snippets of information, photographs, and above all the discovery that Herb had kept a diary.

They hand the diary to me, its small and square and worn around the edges. The early pages are inhabited by a green spidery scrawl which is faded with age. Later pages are in black ink in a firmer hand, as if the writer had grown in confidence.

My focus returns to Herb, he is talking about his beloved bomber, the City of Monroe, just as if he was still there. He is sitting in a cramped space located adjacent to the navigator and around a blind corner behind the upper gun turret; there are no windows. It's cramped and claustrophobic and the dangers all around are unseen.

An explosion, the plane rocks, bucks, flak is searing its way through the fragile fabric of the fuselage, loose items are flying around bouncing off Herb's head, darkness…

I am back 60 years ago – it's hot, there are flashes of light, I'm scared – the stench of burning flesh is creeping into every part of the plane, into every part of me, into my soul. Help me…

"Mike, Mike are you alright?"

It's Ron, he's standing over me shaking my shoulder. "Yes, yes", I tell him, "I'm fine".

I knew at that moment that we needed to take the reader back to experience the reality of war not from a historical perspective, but that of a 23-year old frightened boy.

This book has four authors, the most important two being Staff Sergeant Herbert L. Greer speaking in 1945 from his diary as a young man of 23, and Herb Greer as a not quite so young 83 year-old. To help things along the way Ron Greer, Herb's son, spent four years interviewing his dad, meeting the people Herb flew with, and extensively researching the period. More recently Mike Wicks came along to bring an objective eye to the project and help pull all the elements together.

What makes this book special is the fact that we hear directly from Herb as a 23 year-old through the written passages of his diary and then we have the 83 year-old Herb talking with the authors. Remarkably, the two perspectives are not substantially different, but they do provide a unique opportunity for him to expand, elaborate and give further insight into a fascinating period of history that fashioned the world we know today.

As you read this book you will clearly see that the type (the font), changes to reflect who is speaking.

As this book goes to print we as a nation memorialize this year 2005 as the 60th Anniversary of the end of World War II.

INTRODUCTION

President Harry S. Truman said "It's the small events, unnoticed at the time, that later are discovered to have changed history." Since the Pacific war in the early 1940's many stories have emerged about the men and their battles. Each story, perhaps on its own, goes unnoticed, seemingly inconsequential, but in retrospect they all played a significant role in the final outcome of the victory over Japanese forces.

This is the story of the last few months of World War II in the Pacific, seen through the eyes of one man, a radio operator who kept a diary. The diary tells of the horrors of war. It was written in darkness, and often fear, with a pen-light during lonely hours confined in a space no bigger than a closet, for up to 18 hours at a time. Our main author, cold, frightened and sitting on up to 20,000 pounds of jellied gasoline, while blindly flying through constant flak bursts and fighter opposition, is the subject of this book.

It is not a history book in the true sense of the term, although it does provide its fair share of dates, facts and figures. It is more about the contribution made by one man, and through him the story of the contribution made by all those who fought for our freedom, especially those who flew in the B-29 Superfortress' over the Pacific.

This personal view of the Pacific war gives us two perspectives, separated by 60 years. The first is the story of an airman and the many battles he fought to give us the freedom we enjoy today - it is the story of Staff Sergeant Herbert L. Greer, a radio operator aboard a B-29 bomber told from the pages he wrote in his diary at the age of 23, and then, the second perspective, recounted from his armchair 60 years later. A survivor among so many casualties telling his story lest it be lost forever; one more piece in a jigsaw puzzle that will never, and should never, be finished. A story of his fight for our freedom.

Make no mistake, freedom is NOT free. More than 30,000 WWII veterans die every month and more than 75% of those who fought in the war are now dead. There are fewer and fewer left to tell their stories. This is the story of a survivor of 28 bombing missions during WWII and more than 30 in Korea.

PART I

THE EARLY YEARS

CHAPTER ONE:

Herb was born September 25th, 1921 to Fred L. Greer and Nellie D. Greer in Chelan, Washington, a small town of about 2,000 people. Over the next ten years the town was to see its population grow, and by 1930 some 2,484 souls lived there. Chelan lies at the southern tip of Lake Chelan (pronounced Sha-lan) which means beautiful water in the language of the Chelan Indians. Chelan is 159 miles from Seattle and 93 miles from Yakima.

Lake Chelan is known today, as it was in the early 1920s, for its orchards and particularly for its Red Delicious apples. Washington State produces more than half of all eating apples in the United States and its orchards, nestled in the foothills of the Cascade mountain range, cover 174,000 acres.

Herb's father and his father's brothers, along with Herb's grandfather, purchased an apple orchard in Quincy, Washington, located approximately 50 miles from Wenatchee, which by many is considered the apple capital of the world. They were happy running the orchard for several years until one night a severe frost caught everyone, including the weather bureau, off guard. Without a warning weather forecast, farmers hadn't anticipated the need for "Smudge pots" to counter the freezing conditions, so unfortunately they lost their entire crop. Smudge pots were heaters that pumped out thick black smoke, casting a pall over the orchard that reflected infrared radiation, trapping enough heat between the cloud of smoke and the ground to stop the delicate buds from freezing. Farmers would burn old tires and used motor oil in the pots. Unfortunately the smoke was both a health and an environmental hazard so by 1950 the use of Smudge pots was starting to be regulated.

Unable to recover from this setback Herb's family sold the orchard to a company in Wenatchee and moved to Grand Coulee Washington where Herb's father found work helping to build the Grand Coulee Dam. Once the dam was completed the family moved to Redding California where Herb's father went to work as a mechanic for the highway department and his mother was a laundry worker. Herb, the oldest of seven children, had three brothers, Don, Frank and Harry, and three sisters, Shirley, Darlene and Dallas.

I was quite a handful as a kid and I can remember breaking the headlight on our car with a rock before I was five. On that occasion my father saw to it that I couldn't sit down for a week!

I can remember Don and I were quite the mischievous pair when we were around five and six, especially when we got bored. One of the things we started doing was standing nails just behind the tires of visitors' cars. The anticipation of them having a flat tire on the journey made us giggle like crazy. Of course it wasn't long before my parents put two and two together and realized that all these flat tires only occurred after people had visited us. Then you know what really hit the fan – and I don't mean feathers! We got paddled well and thoroughly on that occasion, but I suppose it saved us down the line from more serious penalties.

Apparently when I was very young I used to answer everything with "huh?" If mom called it was "huh?"—nothing else. It drove my mom crazy. I haven't changed a lot in all these years; I'm told I still use the term on occasion. Unlike most other kids whose first words are traditionally "Momma" or Daddah" I think mine was a non-gender specific "Huh?"

When I was seven, something happened that was to change my life and set me on a path that would determine what would be the central theme of my life – flying.

Out of a clear blue sky my brother Don and I heard a droning sound that became louder and louder, then we saw two specks in the distance, which got bigger and bigger as the drone became a roar. We ran three miles to get closer and then we saw them, our destiny – although neither of us knew it at the time – two army bi-planes had landed in a wheat field. Little did I know, they had cast a spell over me. I was in awe and became driven to discover everything I could about these wonderful machines, and to see places that I could only imagine in my wildest dreams.

It was some time later when my father's friend, Burley Nix, the owner of the local Buick dealership, invited my dad and I to fly in his single engine, two-seater Eaglerock biplane with its large wooden propeller and wire wheels.

My dad encouraged my mother, my brother Don and me to take a spin. In those still fairly early days of flight you had to be quite a brave soul to risk going up in one of these contraptions but, like most kids, fear doesn't play a major role in most decisions and when we got a chance to go up in this beautiful machine we jumped at the chance. We took off two miles outside of Spokane, Washington and soared like an eagle over the county where all the houses and farms became insignificant dots and the only thing that mattered was the wind in our hair and a sense of exhilaration that left us wanting more. I had taken the first step toward my dream. From the moment we were in the air we knew that this was going to be part of our life forever.

It wasn't unusual for people in rural areas to get the opportunity to fly in those days. As part of Eaglerock's promotional campaign, "barnstormers" would travel across rural America and land in fields charging people anything from 50¢ to a dollar for the opportunity to take a flight.

The Eaglerock was the creation of the Alexander Aircraft Company in Englewood, Colorado and was at the time considered to be state of the art. Even Lindbergh had considered using it for his New York to Paris flight. However the company was so busy with orders it was unable to meet his schedule.

By the time I was eight we lived on an apple orchard and our world revolved around apples. My father, his brothers and my granddad owned it. The area was famous for its Red Delicious apples – they were large deep vibrant red, sweet and delicious. In the early spring the orchard would come to life and we would begin spring cleaning, clearing all the prunings and other brush from beneath the trees. Pieces of wood, dried grass and other bits and pieces would be piled in an area and then burnt, the sweet smell of burning apple wood permeating the air.

This was also a time to fertilize the land and trees, a time of anticipation. By May the new buds were blossoming with their sweet perfume-like smell and the farm came alive with activity.

They were good days – I used to go round in bare feet wearing overalls – my first uniform!

It was quite a good life, but we weren't rich gentleman farmers. It was tough for my parents to make a living and keep all us kids fed and clothed. I remember that haircuts were the traditional kitchen bowl-on-the-head variety – one size fits all!

Once the trees started to bloom the orchard would be a riot of beautiful white blossoms, buzzing with industrious, friendly bees. Their job of pollinating the trees was so important that my father used to rent hives to ensure there were enough of the fellows to get the job done.

I used to walk to school most days, although occasionally I could catch a ride on one of the trucks. My school uniform was my overalls – it seems that my whole childhood was spent in those dungarees! I used to take an apple and a mashed 'brown bean' sandwich for lunch everyday.

As I got older I started to work in the orchard. It was expected of me, as I was the oldest child.

When the apple crop was getting close to harvesting time, Herb would make apple boxes out of wood. He would work all day nailing these boxes together. This was a long job as he would have to help make enough for the entire apple crop. The money earned wasn't spent on luxuries—it went towards new shoes, underwear, overalls and if he did really well he might have enough for a new winter coat.

Many times my brother Don would stack the boxes and bring the raw materials for box making. That way, when I finished a box, I had the material available to start on another. This helped us to maximize the number of boxes we could make each day. When, on occasion, we went to town on the weekend we were sometimes each given 50 cents to spend. When we went to visit an uncle or aunt on a long weekend, we occasionally received up to $1 to spend. When we had a dollar in our pocket we felt as though we were rich and could buy the world, or at least a good portion of it. On birthdays we would negotiate the amount of money to be spent on presents.

Our old Chevy sedan didn't have a heater, so during the winter if we had to travel any distance, my father would heat a fairly large rock, either on the iron stove or over the coal-burning furnace, and place it on the rear floor of the vehicle. This would help us to stay reasonably warm, at least for part of the trip.

I learned early on that a good work ethic was expected of me and I worked hard on the farm. This doesn't mean to say that I was a perfect kid. When you grow up on a farm you develop a lot of rough edges that kids more traditionally brought up in town don't necessarily have.

We weren't squeamish for a start – nature was there to be tamed and undesirable critters were likely to take the food out of your mouth, so early on I learned how to use a .22 rifle. We would walk six to eight miles a day hunting cottontail rabbits and had no compunction about shooting them for dinner. Some animals were pests and it was our job to keep their numbers down. Chicken hawks were a constant threat around the chicken houses especially if there were baby chicks around, and were definitely fair game. Rattlesnakes too needed culling for obvious reasons. A kid living on a farm has to pull his weight and these little things made a difference. We didn't kill for killing's sake though and left harmless critters like bull snakes and black snakes in peace, as they were not the enemy.

There are a few things I did as a kid that I look back on and think perhaps they had a hand in hardening my future attitude. As I said, life on a farm is down-to-earth and a lot of the time you found yourself facing reality head on. We had a different view on pests and it wasn't always very humane. For instance, I remember the time we went up to one of the horses and stole a hair from its tail. This had to be done with great care if you didn't want to end up taking an unexpected and painful flight across the barnyard. Now a horse's tail hair is long and strong, but still fairly thin and we threaded it through a kernel of dried corn that we had carefully drilled a hole through, and tied it on securely. The other end we nailed to the roof of the workshop. Then we waited until Mr. Magpie came along and gobbled it up. He was then trapped! At this point a hired hand walking by saw what we were doing and told us to hang on to the bird and that he would take care of it. A few minutes later he returned with a dynamite cap and about six to eight inches of fuse. He then joined the fuse and magpie together using the reverse procedure to how we got the horse's tail hair and tossed the bird into the air. The bird took to the wing instantly and a few seconds later a loud blast and the wide distribution of feathers announced that another farm pest had bitten the dust.

Although it was mostly farm pests that bore the brunt of our adolescent brutality, we occasionally teased the billy goats by inserting Lady Fingers[1] into their rear ends and then lighting them. We found the resulting scene of old Billy snorting and galloping across the yard highly amusing. Of course this was usually a one-time performance as they were usually pretty skittish about any further contact with us.

There was always a clear line between friend and foe for me even as a child. Looking back, I suppose this was some early conditioning, preparing me for my life in the war. Enemies had to be dealt with whatever way you could. It was them or us – and it wasn't going to be us.

For a while Don and I hunted gophers. They would dig holes and burrows in the irrigation ditches and these holes would divert water that was much

[1] Small firecrackers

needed by the trees. This meant that the farmers had to hire extra men to continually walk the orchard finding and repairing the holes. This led local growers to put a bounty on these incorrigible critters that offered 5¢ for each left ear. This turned into quite a little business for us. We would lay traps in the gopher holes and then go back later and if we had captured any we would then make sure that they never did anymore digging! With a bag full of left ears for our trouble we would present ourselves at the end of the day and get paid. All went well until in the true tradition of entrepreneurship we thought about how we could increase our profitability. I can't remember whether it was Don or I who thought of it, but we decided we could double our profit if we presented both ears for payment, after all who could tell the difference between a left and right ear anyway? Of course it didn't take long for our employer to catch on to what we were doing and that was the end of a beautiful business partnership.

COUNTDOWN TO WAR

CHAPTER TWO

Herb's school life was pretty much that of the average All-American kid; he played baseball and basketball, skipped a few lessons, had crushes on sweet redheads and not so sweet blondes, got disciplined, and missed homework deadlines. The difference however, was that he had to leave school during the tenth grade and go to work. The Great Depression era was economically tough on most American families, and his was no exception. He was the oldest and knew where his responsibilities lay. This pattern of sacrifice would repeat itself as the world moved inexorably towards war.

In Grand Coulee he worked as a mechanic in a service station. At the age of seventeen, he became a jackhammer operator on the Grand Coulee Dam. The dam had been started in 1933 and is an amazing feat of engineering and sheer hard labor. There is enough concrete in the dam to build a 3,000 mile, four lane highway clear across the United States, and the base of the dam is almost four times larger than the base of the Great Pyramid of Giza!

Herb's work on the dam ironically produced most of the electricity for the Boeing Aircraft plant which built that big beautiful bomber the B-29 Superfortress and prepared him for his next challenge which was to work on building the Dutch Harbor naval, air and submarine base in Alaska. So there he was, still a teenager, working on Umnak Island, 800 miles southwest of Anchorage in the Aleutians. It was a tough life, often working ten hours a day, seven days a week with no overtime until he had worked forty-eight hours straight. He wrote the following letter back to his family on July 16, 1941.

> I went to work today, worked ten hours, and boy I didn't stand around either. What I mean, we really worked and I am going to work ten hours seven days a week. Between working, eating and sleeping, you don't have a lot of time fooling around up here. I got a big gash in the bottom of my left foot last Monday morning July 13th. It hurts like the devil and I can't hardly walk on the damn foot but I think I'll make it. I worked today so I think I'll live through it. Got me a pair of breeches, and am buying a pair of rubber boots from my roommate. Boy you sure need them here. Whenever it rains the wind blows like the devil, if you don't think it isn't wet, just stand in the rain when the wind is blowing and see. It's a tough one here, but I'm going to be just a little tougher. Some of the fellows are leaving as soon as they can get enough money saved to leave on, but not me. Clarence has got a terrible cold, just about got him down, but he is still kicking. Says he thinks he'll make the grade, doesn't care much whether he does or not, he says. We are staying in government barracks with about 50 other men. We eat in a big mess hall which has four big tables and seats about 200 men, darn good eats though. I am going to work driving truck that pays $1.47 and time and half for all overtime over 48 hours. We are staying in "Unalaska," a

little village about two miles from the base. We ride back and forth in a government boat free of charge. How is all the kids getting along? Tell Harry hello for me. Tell Don hello and tell him to write. I sent some post cards when we left Kodiak, they should be there by now. How is Betty? How is she behaving, how did she feel about me leaving the night I left. Write and tell me how things are getting along. Tell me about Betty, I kind of miss the little devil, I don't know whether she would speak to me now after reading that letter I left her. Would you send me a pair of those house slippers like Harry got Fred for Christmas. Pop still working, sure is lots of work here, but this is no place for a married man. Most of the men that are leaving are married. I am sending the Kodak back, little later on, can't have one here on the island. It's at the marine headquarters now along with about 100 more of them. Can get it anytime I want too, if I sent it home. Won't get paid until Sunday 27th, so won't be able to send any money for about a month. First check will be a small one anyhow. Goodbye now, I'll be seeing you.

Love, Herb

Please write as soon as you can and <u>don't forget.</u>

Herb sent home three out of every four paychecks, once again proving that he knew, even as a teenager, where his responsibilities lay. Luckily, by the time Dutch Harbor was attacked by the Japanese in early June 1942 Herb was long gone. The bombardment lasted for two days and resulted in 43 American deaths. He was terminated for, as he puts it "moving a building". In his own words:

I was driving a 1941 Ford tandem-axle Dump Truck loaded with rock at about 1:00 am in the morning. I had been driving 32 hours straight and had just delivered a load of material from a vessel at the dock. I went to the rock quarry to pick up another load of rock which they were using for foundation on the road, when I fell asleep at the wheel. I was undoubtedly dreaming that my brakes had failed when I drove straight into a building. It was only later that I learned that I had failed to negotiate a corner and ran right into the two-story building; the force of the impact actually moved it slightly to the right. They told me they had to use a pry bar to move the cab out of my lap in order to pull me from the truck. Amazingly

I only received a cut on one finger - my lunch box, which was on the passenger side of the cab on the floor, was not so lucky and was mashed flat. I was later informed that I had been released from my job and was free to return to the States. I can only assume my supervisor was not interested in moving any more buildings.

THE
TRAINING
YEARS

CHAPTER THREE

Throughout the latter part of 1941 Herb and his brother Don watched the war in Europe with interest. The memory of the Eaglerock aircraft was still fresh in their minds and both had the urge to fly. Joining the armed forces seemed like an ideal way to make their dream come true, so in the early part of 1942 they both applied to the War Training Service (WTS) to learn to fly. The WTS was previously the Civilian Pilot Training Program. They took the test in Spokane but unfortunately both failed.

On November 8, 1942 Herb was drafted and thus began his new life in the U.S. Army, which at that time included the air corps; interestingly the United States Air Force did not come into being as a separate, stand-alone arm of the U. S. Military until September 18, 1947.

Herb was sent to Jefferson Barracks in Missouri for his basic training and there got a taste of what army life was like. Discipline was tough but Herb continued to show that with a little ingenuity, you could make life a whole lot easier on yourself.

I learned early on to keep a coffee can under my bunk. This prop was highly useful. When we were called out for work detail I used to hold it under my arm and as long as I had it I was never questioned as to where I was going or what I was doing. The can was used for picking up trash or cigarette butts and in this way I could wander all over the base.

You had to be smarter than the Sergeants if you didn't want to end up with a tough job. I remember once a Sergeant asking if any of us had truck driving experience, the numbskulls who put up their hands thinking that this could be a cushy job ended up being assigned a wheel-barrow to drive.

One of the worst assignments was kitchen police (KP) in the dining hall. We had to scrub the floors with lye soap until the wood was white. Of course it was never good enough and the old mess sergeant would take one look at it and tell us it wasn't clean and we had to start over. I also think I peeled enough potatoes to feed the entire U.S. for a day, with enough left over to make a good batch of vodka.

I think I spent most of my time at Jefferson Barracks drilling. It seemed that we just drilled and drilled and drilled and for the rest of the time we got yelled at! At inspection our Sergeant would get right in our faces and yell – at first I thought I had been wrongly assigned to a hearing impaired group!

They would pick up on the smallest thing and yell at you. One soldier had a thread showing out of his pocket. This was enough for the Sergeant to accuse him of growing rope. It was tough and demoralizing but I suppose it was the standard method of completely demoralizing you so that they could bring you back up to a point where you would obey instructions without even thinking. How well it worked, or whether there might have been a better method I'm not sure. Personally I was always looking for ways to circumvent the system – and usually found them too!

It was certainly tough, as it was obviously intended to be. We slept in tents with wooden floors. They were pretty cold and inhospitable but at least they had wooden sides that came up about four feet from the floor which made them a little less drafty.

We were always looking for ways to escape to town, even when we didn't have a pass. I remember on one occasion we were just coming back from a trip to town and had climbed over the fence. A few feet inside camp we noticed that a guard had spotted us – quick as a flash we acted as if we were heading toward the fence. He of course ordered us back thinking that we were attempting to leave the base. Our hangdog expressions as we strolled back to our barracks assured him he was correct and nothing more was said. Friday night we went into town, East St.Louis, which is actually in Illinois and not Missouri which is a little confusing, but not as much as the sign we saw in the yard of a home that stated 'No Soldiers or Dogs Allowed'. We weren't sure how to take that, but we got a laugh out of it. Imagine a dog that can read! Anyway at least we got top billing!

Once Herb had completed basic training he was shipped to Scott Field, Illinois where he was to spend three months. He was half way through radio school when he again had the opportunity to take the exam for pilot training. This time he passed and was shipped to Santa Ana, California for primary schooling. About a month into the program he was called before the training board and was informed he had washed out. It was his lack of adequate math skills that was his undoing. His early departure from school to work to support the rest of the family meant he did not have the basic math knowledge to be able to cope with the academic demands of the course.

He was reassigned to gunnery school and sent to Kingman, Arizona. He was by this time becoming quite a well-traveled young man.

It was at Kingman that Herb got his military issue diary out and started to keep his journal. It was tentative at first, the work of a young man trying to find something to say, and perhaps feeling a little self-conscious about putting his thoughts down on paper.

The very first entry actually addresses the diary, which makes one think that perhaps when he took it up he was feeling lonely and in need of someone, or something, to talk to.

July 16, 1943

Dear diary, I guess I am kind of late getting you started. I will have been in the service a year August 4, 1943. I came into the army in Fort Lewis, Washington August 4, 1942. I was sent to Jefferson Barracks, Missouri for my basic training. From J. B. I was sent to Scott Field, Illinois where I went to radio operator and mechanic school. Upon finishing I was sent to Santa Ana, California as a Cadet where I stayed through preflight. I was washed out because of my math & physics not being up to par. From there I was sent to Fresno, California where I was reclassified as an aircraft gunner while being stationed there. I got a seven day furlough and went home, which was really heaven and I ain't kidding. I'm now at Kingman, have been here about 7 weeks in which the first week I done my share of K.P. I was in the hospital 2 weeks with the flu but feel fine now. I'm in school again and doing fine. Shot skeet the last four days and is my shoulder sore. I just received word today that my cousin Robert Greer went overseas. I hope to be over helping him out soon as I can. Guess that is all for tonight, bye now.

Herb's entries, during this period, were quite brief; often in their brevity can be read his frustration; such as on 22 July, 1943 when he sums up his day with five words, *"Same old routine as yesterday."*

During the middle of July he talks of parades that were, in his words, *"a flop"* and implies that this was usual at Kingman Gunnery School.

On 18 July 1943 he writes, *had a little fun today, went up in the mountains to Wallapine Lodge to go swimming and get a load of rocks. We went and got the rocks and it was raining like hell, so we never got to swim. I was soaked when I got back."*

The rocks were used on the side of each walkway on the Army Air Base or the areas that were restricted. They were painted white. As Herb says, *"In these days if you can't pick it up then you paint it white."*

He talks about meeting a girl at the Post Exchange, but states that he is not interested and complains about the rain.

It is obvious that he is bored and frustrated at this point.

Monday 19 July, 1943

Today we shot moving base skeet, but my right shoulder was so darn sore I couldn't sleep with it, so I shot left handed and got a better score than I ever have. Nothing else of importance, just same old routine.

For the next several days every entry in the diary complains of *"the same old routine"* even after shooting skeet from a turntable mounted with shotguns. He mentions getting a letter from Shirley, but we never get to know what it said. Herb, even as a young man, was not prone to discussing his personal life or innermost feelings. It is when he achieves, or masters something that he feels compelled to talk to his diary about it, as on 23 July when he says, *"Had to take every part off the .50 caliber that would come off and in the dark too."*

The following day he mentions that he was on K.P., but quickly states *"not punishment,"* lest his family should read this at a later date.

Characteristically he follows this with some self-deprecating humor when he writes, *"The squadron won the parade today, so I guess it must have been that I wasn't there to mess it up ha! ha!"*

We must not forget however that although Herb was a somewhat serious fellow he was still a very young man, as the following entry indicates.

Sunday 25 July, 1943

Had quite a time today. We all went up on Wallapine on a big beer bust because of the class going into "air to air" soon. Had cases of beer and I got my share too. Other than having one car roll over twice and one guy fall from a truck, and one guy fall from a bluff, the day went by reasonably good.

It is interesting to note that even though they rolled a car and someone fell from a bluff it was still a reasonable day! This is a good example of how young people feel immortal.

The next few days were spent in gunnery training, save of course, for the occasional day sweeping sand out of the barracks. His entry for 27 July talks excitedly about firing from a Ball Turret and firing a hand-held .50 caliber. The Ball Turret hung down from beneath the airplane and was extremely cramped. So much so that the gunner would often not be able to wear a parachute. He was also completely isolated from the rest of the crew. It was an unenviable job but, contrary to common belief, actually quite safe. Statistics show that in terms of fatalities the Ball Turret gunner had the safest job; the pilot's being the most dangerous.

The weather at Kingman left a lot to be desired and Herb complained to his diary, *We had a dust storm this evening. It was so thick you couldn't see 3 feet ahead of you and it ended raining so damn hard, it almost flooded the place out. Well guess that is all for now."*

As the month comes to a close Herb mentions the days of firing practice and shows concern about whether his scores are high enough. He states, *"I did quite well on time firing, however the night firing was not what I had hoped for."* He also recalls that he was amazed that after taking apart and reassembling a .50 caliber blindfolded he was quite amazed when it actually fired!

Saturday 31 July, 1943

On the range this morning and I only got 8 hits out of 200 with cal. 30 machine gun. Our swimming pool opened today, boy I sure had a time swimming and they had a few beers there too, what a time wow! I don't know if I gotten enough hits or not, if I have I go into air to air Monday. I got my fingers crossed. Bye now.

He is still talking to his diary, and is still concerned with his scores, but on the last day of July he seems to be enjoying himself a little. And, as we enter August he has wangled his way onboard an aircraft and is in his element riding in the nose.

Monday 2 August, 1943

Our first day in air to air today but I lost my first mission. We were all in the plane and taxied down the runway to take off and then developed engine trouble. Both engines were losing RPM's. We taxied back to the hangar, but when we got ready to exchange ships, we got orders that all ships were grounded because of low overcast. But I fooled them, I hooked me a ride in an AT 11 and we went up towards Boulder. Rode out in the nose, good view there, it is fiberglass (guess that's all). Hope we have more luck in flying today.

The early part of August is spent in practice as he fires from a Martin turret in a Lockheed AT-18, (nicknamed the Hudson), at a target being towed by a North American AT-6 (the Texan).

On 6 August he states that *"This army life is killing me."* There is no explanation and perhaps none is necessary.

The following day Herb's time at Kingman comes to an end and he is moved to Yucca, southeast of Las Vegas for his last week of air to air training. It was a satellite airfield for the use of Kingman Army Air Field (AAF) and its gunnery school.

As soon as he arrives he complains of the heat *"Got here at Yucca last night, done nothing today, but it's around 110 degrees in the shade."*

Once active again, Herb seems happier, as his diary entry for Monday 9 August states:

Monday 9 August, 1943

Began first firing from an AT-6 today, boy sure gives a guy a thrill firing from the rear cockpit. Peel off about 1200 feet above the target and fire at it as we go by. Is it ever hard to stand up, with plenty of slipstream to battle against.

A few days later he comments that he fired 200 rounds, they lost their target and his pilot got into a sham combat with another aircraft and he had *"...a grand time trying to hang on. We cut more shines than a monkey on a flag pole."*

Herb obviously enjoyed his taste of mock combat because a few days later, after firing another 200 rounds, his pilot cut loose and dove from 10,000 feet to about 1,200 and Herb writes, *"...boy what a ride."*

On the thirteenth of the month he fires his last 200 rounds and is praying that his score is high enough. As it turns out, he need not have worried as he graduates gunnery school on 16 August, gets his diploma and immediately goes from a "slick sleeve" to a three-stripe Buck Sergeant.

Upon graduation at gunnery school Herb was shipped with other graduates to Salt Lake City where he was assigned to a crew.

> *Our new crew was shipped to Clovis, New Mexico where we were assigned a new B-24 J model bomber. We flew several training missions here.*

> *I remember getting prepared for one mission where we were on the flight line along with several other aircraft all with their engines running. The noise was deafening and there was a lot of people moving back and forth checking things. The navigator of the B-24 next to us must have gotten confused or distracted and accidentally backed into the propeller. The B-24 has a high wing; thus the engine is quite high as well. I could see how, if you were not paying attention, it would be easy not to notice exactly where you were positioned unless you were looking directly up. Needless to say, he didn't survive this encounter.*

Once Herb finished training at Clovis the crew was sent to Alamogordo for advanced training. At this point fate took a hand and changed the war for Herb. He caught pneumonia and was hospitalized while the rest of his crew was shipped to Europe. Another radio operator took his place and that was the last he saw of his new buddies; he never did find out whether they made it back or not.

> *Once I was released from the hospital they made me an instructor on both B-24's and B-29's. So for the time being, Alamogordo became home.*

> *The only time I ever actually crashed was in training. It was also the only time I was injured, except for a few bumps and bruises during some of the more boisterous missions. It was a routine training flight where we had a student pilot with an instructor pilot and a student radioman with myself as his instructor. There were also student gunners accompanied by instructor gunners. We had gone through all the procedures carefully as you would expect when teaching students and were thundering down the runway with everything going smoothly when, just as we reached the point of no return, we lost number three engine, which was not a good thing. A few seconds later we lost number four and were in serious trouble. We reached an altitude of approximately 150 feet and did not achieve the step to fly and we crashed about two miles from the runway in a field. The engines hit first and fires started immediately. Thank God that it didn't happen on Guam because once you reached the point of no return the next*

thing was the cliff, the rocks and the sea and that combination was not kind to an aircraft or its occupants.

Remarkably we all managed to get out of the plane once it had stopped sliding. An ambulance screamed down the runway and into the field and took us to the hospital. I injured my knee; it still hurts – although now 60 years later – they call it rheumatoid arthritis!

During the crash a coffee jug bounced off the side of the aircraft and spilled on my lap. Of course Major Jones, the training commander of West Wing (not in the White House!) took one look at this and said "what's the matter Greer, did it scare you?" Defending myself from a reputation that could have haunted me for the rest of the war, I explained about the coffee jug. He believed me but was far more interested in expressing his sense of humor.

Once we had all been checked over and released, thankfully with no serious injuries, we decided to go to town and consume as much beer as we could. We didn't return until the early hours and next morning were certainly the worse for wear when we reported for the briefing session. Major Jones took one look at the sorry spectacle we presented and told us we were unfit to fly and directed us to sick call. Unbeknown to us he had told the flight surgeon to give us all a healthy dose of castor oil. He then proceeded to have all the toilet paper removed from the crappers. You can imagine how the story played out from there!

Of course, nothing remains the same for long in the military, especially during wartime, so I wasn't too surprised when three or four months later I was picked to join a new crew, this time on a B-29. Apparently an Aircraft Commander had become very ill and was going to be hospitalized for an extended period of time. Major Jones volunteered to take this fellow's aircraft over on condition he could pick his own crewmembers.

Major Luther Jones was to be an important factor in Herb's survival of the war. For his new crew he picked mostly instructors, as they would not need to undertake advance training and were all experts in their own fields. This would prove to make for an exceptionally strong team.

Although Major Jones was without doubt a great pilot there was one occasion where he had a little trouble getting his plane down on the ground. Tim Holt, our bombardier and Hollywood Star, decided that he would try to get us some entertainment for the Christmas holiday. To this end we were allowed to take a B-17G to Los Angeles airport so that Tim could speak to his rich and famous friends. All was well until Major Jones attempted to land at LA without making an adjustment for the fact that the airport was at sea level, not a few thousand feet above sea level like Alamogordo. As the plane approached the runway it appeared to want to continue to fly and after four or five touch downs, Flight Officer Marshall Goldston, our Engineer, asked the Major if he would like to divide up the landings with the co-pilot. It is fair to say that Major Jones did not share Goldston's sense of humor at that particular moment.

Undoubtedly the person who had the biggest impact on Herb was Major Luther Jones. Luther Jones was born in Epps, Louisiana December 7, 1917, making him only 27 years of age during their missions over Japan. His father was a cotton farmer, but it was a tough living so they moved to Monroe, Louisiana in November 1923 where his father became a carpenter. When Luther was 13 the family went back to farming. Luther graduated high school and went to Northeast Louisiana Junior College in Clark, Louisiana where he studied math and science. However, in his second year he was told that he needed to pass a course on Shakespeare to graduate, so he opted to transfer to Louisiana Tech where he could further his interest in airplanes, or his disinterest in Shakespeare, he never really said. In his first year he enrolled in flight training and later earned his license in a Piper Cub airplane. Who knew at the time that he would quickly move on from that tiny plane to pilot the largest airplane ever built?

Soon after, he entered the Army Air Corps at Maxwell, Alabama and later became an instructor pilot on AT6 aircraft. A year later, in 1941, he was flying twin-engine aircraft and then graduated to the B-17 Flying Fortress. From that point it was inevitable that he would be instrumental in taking the B-29 to the enemy. In 1943 he was moved to Clovis and then Alamogordo, New Mexico where he became the B-29 instructor and Commander of West Training Area.

It felt good to be hand picked and to be one of a crew of experts. Major Jones was known to be a first-rate pilot and I felt that we were all in safe hands. About a week later, we traveled by train to Kearney, Nebraska to pick up our new B-29 and then we were off to who knew where overseas.

*Before we left however, I had time to marry the sweetest girl in
Alamogordo, her name was Hazel Jean Ozbirn and she was a clerk typist at
the base. So, newly married, there I was going off to war in one of the new
B-29's with a star-studded crew. Scary but exciting. I was 23 years old and
a married man. Hazel Jean returned home to her folks in Salem, Arkansas
to wait out the war, and hopefully my return.*

Herb's other sweetheart was to be the B-29, an amazing aircraft that
would take him into the heart of the action and bring him back safely.

QUEEN OF THE SKIES

CHAPTER FOUR

The men who were carried in her belly on the significant WWII bombing missions over Japan, called the B-29 the "Cadillac" of airplanes. They were bigger, heavier, faster, flew farther and were more technologically advanced than anything else that had ever been built, and are now hailed as one of the industrial miracles of the early 1940's. The Army Air Corps were so impressed with the concept they ordered 250 of the new bombers, even though they existed only on paper. The B-29 came along at

a time when long-range bombing of any kind was impossible because of the limitations of existing aircraft. Without that strategic ability, it seemed unlikely that victory over a country like Japan, surrounded by thousands of miles of ocean, was possible. In fact, the Japanese high command had boasted that Tokyo was beyond the reach of any land-based air bombers and considered it untouchable.

With Japan becoming an increasing threat, the United States Army Air Corps challenged several aircraft manufacturers in early 1940 to come up with a bomber that could fly at 400 mph, with a range of more than 5,300 miles, which had the capability of carrying a bomb load weighing 20,000 lbs. for at least half of that distance. Boeing won the contract with its design for the B-29, a plane that would ultimately play a decisive role in bringing an end to the war in the Pacific.

In August of 1943, the allied leaders met in Quebec, Canada to discuss the defeat of Japan. Japan's threat had been looming since the late 1920's because of its incredible industrial strength. Since the attack on Pearl Harbor, Japan had doubled its steel production capacity, and more than tripled its armed forces. Japan also possessed the world's third largest merchant fleet, and showed no signs of slowing down, with new ships being built continuously. It was during these discussions that President Roosevelt brought to the allied discussions the potential of a weapon capable of dealing a blow to Japan's industrial might. This weapon was the B-29 Superfortress and it was built for a single strategic mission: to destroy Japan's military and industrial capabilities. It promised a long-range bombing potential unheard of until then, and made victory over Japan a possibility.

At the time of the talks, only eleven B-29's were in existence, but Roosevelt promised hundreds more. At the time of the first B-29 flight, orders for 1,664 Superfortresses were on the books. It seemed another impossible feat, but Boeing had implemented a revolutionary new construction process, using assembly lines, to construct the aircraft in pieces that could be fitted together at a later date. Altogether, the B-29 contained over 55,000 numbered parts, thousands of miles of wiring and more than 1,000,000 rivets. By 1943, only four months after the allied conference, 35 Superfortresses had come off the assembly line, and by January that number had risen to an astonishing 142. Given the war in

Europe and the Pacific, critical labor shortages were imminent forcing the US to look beyond its current labor force. Women proved to be the answer to the labor problem. At the Boeing Wichita plant, women constituted 39% of the workforce. They were employed as die makers and sheet metal fabricators. The latter involved riveting with guns weighing three to fifteen pounds. This spawned the infamous nickname "Rosie the Riveter." Others occupied positions in drafting, tool making, spot welding, bench work, electrical form assembly as well as many administrative functions. At Boeing's Wichita plant, 2,293 women were hired between August, 1943 and June, 1944. These women, collectively, had 3,671 children. These were difficult times, but the women of America rose to the challenge and forsook their peacetime existence when their country needed them. Their investment was to be a key determining factor in the success of the B-29 production program. By December, 1943, the most ambitious aircraft production program to date was in full swing at Boeing plants in Seattle and in Wichita, Kansas and at Martin and Bell. By 1945, these plants were turning out eight B-29's a day! When manufacturing ceased in 1946, nearly 4,000 Superforts had been delivered.

From the beginning, the B-29 boasted a string of firsts. In the immortal words of General "Hap" Arnold, acting head and future commander of the 20th Army Air Corps, "The difficult we do immediately, the impossible takes a little longer," and the impossible was achieved in the building of the B-29.

Before the first prototype had been constructed, manufacturing facilities had already been established, a risky process that had not been the norm in the aircraft industry. The aircraft was the first to offer innovative features such as pressurized crew compartments. Pressurization meant that the planes needed a remotely controlled gun system since crewmembers couldn't sit in the gun turrets as they did in unpressurized aircraft. In order to meet the Army's requirements for range and bomb load, the B-29 had to be heavy - it was the heaviest production airplane in the world at that time. The bomber also had two bomb bays, which were designed to release bombs alternately to maintain the aircraft's balance.

This enormous flying machine spanned 141 feet 3 inches from wing tip to wing tip and measured 99 feet from nose to tail. Its highest point was the vertical stabilizer on the tail which was 27-feet 9-inches, the height of a three-story building. Despite its size the B-29 was extremely aerodynamic with special attention being paid to the nacelle design to reduce aerodynamic drag, allowing it to fly faster and farther than other aircraft, in spite of its weight. The engine was the completely new 2200 hp Wright R - 3350 Duplex Cyclone eighteen-cylinder twin-row, air-cooled, radial. In order to gain the utmost power at high altitudes, the engine was fitted with two turbo superchargers instead of the usual one. The construction of the aircraft itself was fairly conventional, being made of metal throughout, but with fabric-covered control surfaces. Each undercarriage unit had dual, instead of single wheels, and a retractable tail-skid was provided for protection during nose-high takeoffs and landings. Panels of armor and bulletproof glass protected the pilot and co-pilot, and armored bulkheads protected the gunners in the rear compartments.

The B-29 was equipped with five gun turrets containing a total of twelve machine guns and one canon at the rear (later removed due to performance problems) and once again in the spirit of this new generation flying giant, all the guns were controlled remotely – a first in aviation history. This system allowed more than one gunner to operate more than one turret. The bombardier and each gunner, except the tail gunner, could aim and fire up to two turrets at the same time, if needed. Reflector gun sights were placed at each of the four gunners' and bombardier sighting positions. Each gun sight was wired into the electrical system and sent electrical commands to control, direct, and fire the guns.

The birth of the Superfortress, however, did not come about without labor pains. In the early days it was plagued with chronic engine problems. The engines were subject to chronic overheating and were especially prone to catching fire for no apparent reason. The first B-29 flew on September 21, 1942 at Boeing Field, with Boeing's chief test pilot "Eddie" Allen at the controls. By December, Allen had only been able to get 27 hours in the air from 23 test flights. Sixteen engines had to be changed, nineteen exhaust systems had to be revised, and twenty-two carburetors had to be replaced. And then, on December 28, one of the engines of the prototype caught fire during a test flight, forcing Allen to return immediately to Boeing Field. Things were not looking good. The good news however was, aside from the engine problems, the performance and handling qualities of the B-29 proved to be outstanding, and no significant aerodynamic changes were found to be necessary.

The second B-29 flew for the first time on December 30, 1942, but this flight was also cut short by an engine fire. Further tests were suspended until the engines could be replaced. Interestingly the engines from the first B-29 prototype were removed and put into the second. It flew again on February 18, 1943, but just eight minutes into the flight yet another engine fire broke out, forcing an emergency return to the field. This time things were a whole lot more serious. As Eddie Allen, the brave test pilot, tried to land at Boeing Field, the fire burned through the main wing spar and caused the wing to buckle. The burning aircraft plunged into a nearby meat packing plant killing 20 workers from the plant and everyone on board.

This devastating crash caused enormous concern about the B-29 program. President Roosevelt expressed frustration about the delays to having these giant airplanes on their way to China by the end of 1943 to begin bombing attacks against Japan. At that time, Vice President Harry Truman headed a Special Committee to Investigate the National Defense Program. His committee looked into the B-29 issues and concluded that the problem lay with substandard or defective engines delivered by the Wright Aeronautical Company. In their defense the USAAF admitted to putting too much pressure on the Wright Company to speed up engine delivery.

The third prototype flew for the first time in June of 1943. It incorporated extensive revisions resulting from the experiences with the first two, and was used as the model for setting up mass production at Boeing. It was then handed over to the USAAF for armament and accelerated flight-testing. Although it too later crashed, it did prove that the basic design was sound. In fact, throughout its production history, not a single basic alteration to the airframe was required. This is truly a measure of the fundamental integrity of the aircraft itself, and a tribute to the great super-fortress it was. Of course, to the men who flew her, who treated her as one of the crew and even went down in her, she was far more than just a machine; she was the 12th crewmember.

New pilots of the first B-29's were awestruck by its sheer size and its beauty. They were thrilled to be able to fly such a massive technological feat.

One of the major considerations from the very beginning of the B-29's construction was crew comfort. In smaller bombers, this wasn't an issue - limited range meant less time spent in the aircraft. With the extraordinary range of the Superfortress, the crew could be airborne for up to 18 hours at altitudes of 32,000 feet, where the temperature could drop to 50° below zero. This meant the crew areas would have to be pressurized. The problem was how to open the fuselage to outside air pressure at 32,000 feet in order to drop the bombs. Boeing's solution was to create separate pressurized compartments outside of the double bomb bays, and to connect the two sections with a large tube placed over the top of the bomb bays so airmen could crawl from one section to the other. This ingenious design allowed the crew to fly in pressurized comfort at all times while performing the duties the aircraft was designed to do. The tail gunner had a separate pressurized section of his own.

The crew of the B-29 usually consisted of 11-14 men, who were trained to work together as one, much like fingers on a hand – a team where each member depended completely on the skill and specialist knowledge of the other. In the first compartment at the front of the aircraft and in the transparent nose, sat the bombardier, whose primary job it was to operate the Norden bombsite that put the bombs on the designated target and, equally importantly, operate the lower forward or upper forward gun turrets to protect the plane when threatened by fighter attack. Surrounded in front and on all sides by glass with visibility side to side, up and down, it was like leading a giant from the inside of a bubble.

Behind the bombardier sat the Aircraft Commander and co-pilot. The job of the AC was enormous, beginning with painstaking, detailed pre- and post-flight checks of all the aircraft systems. His in-flight checks were made a great deal more difficult when the aircraft was being shot at, or was experiencing mechanical difficulties. The checks were accomplished with the help of the flight engineer, who monitored the engine RPM, manifold pressure, temperature of the engines, and oil and cabin pressure. This was vital if the aircraft was going to get on and off the ground safely, especially considering the lumbering weight of the beast. The engineer would synchronize and adjust the cowl flaps as needed and once at cruise altitude, fine-tune the engines so that optimal airspeed was reached while economizing fuel. All this continual monitoring was what ensured the aircraft not only reached the target, but got home safely as well. The co-pilot's role was also to carry out a specific series of checks and to assist the pilot with flying the aircraft.

The navigator sat behind the pilot facing forward. An error by him of just 2º could put the crew out over miles of ocean with not enough fuel to finish the mission, or get back to home base safely. The flight engineer sat behind the co-pilot facing the rear of the plane in front of a panel of gauges and instruments. His job was to take care of all four engines of the aircraft while in flight, and with the B-29 that was quite a task. If a system malfunctioned, or there was a fire or power failure, the engineer had to determine what the problem was and how to fix it – quickly! The radio operator took his place behind the engineer facing the right wall in a cramped, windowless section, unable to see anything outside the aircraft. His main function was to send messages or receive them through continuous monitoring of the radio for possible target change, weather updates, distress calls and other reporting. The accuracy and timeliness of his reports were critical for his crew and the entire formation.

In the second compartment (connected to the first by the long pressurized tube) was the CFC (Central Fire Control) gunner who peered through another bubble (known as a blister), which was at the top of the aircraft. He was the only crewmember with a 360º view, from a rotating seat known as the "barber chair." He was depended on to be the "eyes" for what was going on around and above the aircraft. He operated two gun turrets and identified the other gunners' targets, when needed. A left and right gunner sat below the CFC gunner on the right and left sides of the aircraft. They too had transparent blisters to maximize their view. They operated the gun turrets completely by remote control – this was the first time gunners were not actually sitting in the turrets and manually turning the guns toward their target. Behind the gunners was the radar operator who could help with target identification and assist in the bombing run. He also monitored the weather for thunderheads which, if flown into directly, could destroy an aircraft. Finally, in the rear compartment, sat the tail gunner. The rear compartment was not connected to the other two compartments, and the tail gunner, once in flight, only had interphone contact with his crewmates making it the loneliest station on the aircraft. The rear gunner, apart from controlling the rear guns and the canon from his position in the back of the aircraft, also operated the auxiliary power unit. It was affectionately referred to as the putt-putt engine and was used for electrical power during take-off and landing. Although the range of movement of his guns and canon was limited when compared to the other gun turrets, the canon packed an incredible punch, when it functioned properly, to any enemy aircraft trying to attack from the rear.

The operation of the B-29 was extremely complex and depended on each crewmember knowing and doing his job perfectly. Each crewmember's role was critically inter-linked with those of his crewmembers on board, and these men depended on each other for their very lives. The crew tended to become very close, and form a team, or brotherhood. Above all else, each crewmember loved the 12th man, the aircraft; so much so that each plane took on human characteristics, and were given affectionate names by their crew.

The drive to personalize an object is said to be basic to the nature of man, and in times of war, when death has the potential of always being moments away, it seemed even more important to have a sense of belonging and identity – a way to be remembered in case the unthinkable happened. It also became a way to boost the morale of the crews who faced these deadly missions, and the themes of what is now called nose art, were often women. Elaborate paintings representing the chosen names were created on the nose of the B-29's. The paintings were often cartoon-like images of women in various stages of dress (or undress), similar to the sexy "pin-up" girls of the 1940's.

Names like "Dauntless Dotty", "Dixie Babe", "Slick Chicks", "Lucky Lady" and "Pacific Playboys" were chosen. The crews were identified by the name of their B-29, and the image on the side of the aircraft provided for quick and easy identification. When the "Dragon Lady" landed on the airstrip, everyone knew who had made it back safely. Many of the missions have come to be known by the name of the specific aircraft – including the Enola Gay (named after the Aircraft Commander's mother), which carried the first atomic bomb that fell on Hiroshima.

Some controversy arose over these images, many of which were considered to be crude and indecent, and the Army Air Corps tried to restore a sense of decorum with regulations around what should be allowed in these imaginative pieces of art. In an attempt to clean up what was being perceived as indecent and inappropriate representations of the Army Air Corps, crews were encouraged to adopt the name of an American city as their nose art, and many did including Herb and his crew. In an effort to foster greater support and goodwill, images of the US with a flag or pin indicating the location of the city began to appear on the sides of aircraft, in the hopes that fellow Americans in that particular city back home would identify with a specific crew doing battle in the Pacific. Many however, kept the girly images that have since become famous.

In April of 1944 the B-29's headed across the globe where they eventually landed in China. Millions of US dollars had been spent on building and preparing runways and airfields to accommodate the aircraft. WWII film footage shows images of thousands of Chinese workers clearing the area by hauling rock and debris on their backs, in wheelbarrows and hammering rocks into gravel by hand. This agonizing, backbreaking work reaped the Chinese workers a penny per day and was an example of the Chinese support for the Allies and the American war effort. Unfortunately, these airfields were often unusable during bad weather, and created a limited flight range, even for the B-29's, that only touched the lower tip of Japan. American sights turned to the Marianas, a chain of islands consisting primarily of Saipan, Tinian and Guam. They were considered to be ideal bases from which to launch the operations against Japan. The islands were about 1500 miles from Tokyo, a range that was at the outer reaches of what the B-29's could manage. The Marianas, however, were firmly under Japanese control at that time.

General "Hap" Arnold approached the Joint Planning Staff with a proposal for the seizure of the Marianas as early as possible to use them as B-29 bases for the final assault on Japan. Much of the combat that took place over the next two years was over the control of these islands. The islands were declared secure on August 9, 1944, and the US finally had the bases it needed. Much work had to be done to prepare airfields on the islands for the arrival of the B-29's, the first aircraft to fly into Saipan. It was said that "Joltin Josie" was a sensation, who shamelessly stole the show. A local poet present at Josie's landing penned these words:

> On the 12th of October back in 1944
>
> The citizens of Saipan heard a great four-engine roar
>
> Bulldozers fled the runway, the soldiers stopped to cheer
>
> As down came Joltin Josie, the Pacific pioneer

One by one the B-29's arrived, taking their places on Guam, Tinian and Saipan, until there were enough supplies, crews and aircraft to commence the raids on Japan. The distances these missions would cover was unprecedented. The flights from the Marianas to Japan, all over water, were the equivalent of leaving Mexico for targets in Canada. Anticipation and expectations were high for the success of the Superfortresses against Japan. The first few bombing missions however, did not meet expectations.

The target of the first raid against Japan was the Nakajima Aircraft Company's Musashi engine plant, just outside Tokyo. One hundred eleven B-29's, led by Brigadier General Emmet O'Donnell flying "Dauntless Dotty", took off on November 24, 1944. Seventeen of the B-29's had to abort due to another rash of engine failures. The remainder approached the target at altitudes of 27-32,000 feet. For the first time, the B-29 encountered the jet stream, which reared its ugly head at precisely the altitudes at which the bombers were operating. This caused the bomber formations to be disrupted and made accurate bombing impossible. In addition, the pilots encountered cloud cover above the Nakajima plant and only 24 of the B-29's dropped their bombs close to their target. The plant was hardly damaged.

The Musashi plant was revisited ten more times over the next few weeks. The results continued to be disappointing. Only 10% of the damage done by the bombs was actually inside the plant area. Forty bombers had been lost in these eleven raids, many to accidents caused by engine failures. In December of 1944, some five months before Herb's first mission, there were a series of raids against the Mitsubishi engine plant at Nagoya. Although some 17% of the facility was gutted, Japanese defenses were becoming more effective and losses to enemy action were now reaching four or five aircraft per mission.

Concerned about the limited success of the efforts against Japan, General Arnold replaced the then commanding officer – General Hansell – with

General LeMay, and for a time, the bombing raids stopped. General LeMay immediately shifted his attention to a tiny island named Iwo Jima. Located halfway between the Marianas and Japan it was considered an extremely strategic and vital acquisition, as it provided an emergency landing base for aircraft that could not make it all the way to or from Japan due to weather, fuel, or mechanical problems. Iwo Jima was taken, but not before one of the bloodiest battles experienced by U.S. forces, and provided a vital staging post between the Marianas and Japan for the B-29 squadrons. There was also a reduction in fuel consumption as planes did not have to skirt Iwo Jima based enemy fighters. It was later used for American fighter escorts to Japan.

General LeMay began issuing new directives. Upon close analysis of the structure of the Japanese economy, he created new strategies that he felt could turn around the limited success of the B-29 offensive. These strategies took into consideration the targets, and the effects of the jet stream, cloud cover, and high operating altitudes of the B-29 effort. LeMay suggested that high altitude, daylight attacks be replaced by low altitude, high-intensity, incendiary raids at night. This strategy would enable the B-29's to escape the effects of the jet stream and would get the bombers below most of the cloud cover. In addition, the aircraft would no longer have to struggle up to 30,000 feet, saving on fuel and wear on the engines.

The first raid to use these new techniques was on the night of March 9, 1945, against Tokyo. A total of 302 B-29's participated in the raid, with 279 arriving over the target. It lasted for two hours, and was a success beyond anyone's wildest expectations. The individual fires caused by the bombs joined to create a widespread inferno known as a firestorm. When it was over, sixteen square miles of the center of Tokyo had gone up in flames and nearly 84,000 people had been killed. Fourteen B-29's were lost, but it was apparent that these journeys of the giants were starting to make themselves felt and would finally begin to show the significant effect on the war that the US had anticipated.

It is ironic that an aircraft designed to be a high altitude weapons platform, saw its greatest successes at low altitudes, becoming the first, and only, aircraft to effectively end a world war. In fact, after the war, the Japanese military credited the B-29 with being the single most important weapon in their defeat. Altogether, 3,943 Superfortresses were built at a cost of around $600,000 per aircraft. During the war in the Pacific, and later, the Korean War, 362 Superfortresses were lost.

In the early stages of the B-29's development, General Arnold challenged Boeing to:

"Make them the biggest, make them the heaviest, and make them fly the farthest."

And indeed they did. Many believe that history may have been written in an entirely different way if it were not for these amazing flying machines. After all, it is widely known in military circles that "he who controls the air, wins the battle." Without doubt, the B-29's controlled the air over Japan.

PART II
A DIARY OVER JAPAN

The acrid smoke of war lies over the world today. We, who are engaged in this gigantic struggle, are unable to see the future clearly. There is first the victory to be won. The view of the present is un-obscured. We have only daily duties to perform. And we are bound together in full force and determination that come what will the victory shall be ours.

Neither Hun nor Hirohito....nor all the force of evil shall cause us to deviate from this, our great objective. Day by day....night by night we march steadily forward.

And as we fill each unforgiving minute, we advance. And moving with the hands of time each day, draw nearer to the altitude where clearer vision shows the future glorious and sublime. And then, with all production won and distribution solved, we shall in victory stand upon the threshold of peace and plenty everlasting.

So, as we fill each pressing day, we hold within us that divine spark envisioned by our forbearers, that right makes might. We hereby pledge an ever higher plane of living predicated upon the great fundamentals of Democracy and dedicated to the purpose that life, with liberty, shall not perish from the earth.

Taken from a brochure 1st Lt. Tim Holt (Bombardier) made for his parents.

While Herb was preparing for combat assignment the war, both in Europe and the Pacific, was turning in favor of the allies. The United States' forces had invaded Okinawa, the first Japanese home island to be taken. In Europe, the allies were starting to take control in Germany and Italy. American and British soldiers were liberating prisoners in German concentration camps.

President Franklin D. Roosevelt dies and Harry S. Truman becomes the 33rd president of the United States.

Vienna is taken over by Soviet troops and the allies capture Arnhem. A few days later the last of the German soldiers surrender on the Ruhr. In the dying days of April 1945, Benito Mussolini is executed.

The horrors of the Dachau concentration camp, just outside the German city of Munich, are discovered by U.S. troops as they liberate the camp. They find bodies piled everywhere; in the morgue, outside the prisoner's huts, and even in box cars in a nearby railway siding.

On the last day of April, Adolf Hitler and Eva Braun commit suicide in a bunker in Berlin.

But for Herb, saying goodbye to his parents in California, the war is just beginning.

The entries that follow provide a unique insight into the life of a B-29 Radioman. First, through the actual writings in his diary, kept while in the midst of the action, we hear the voice of Staff Sgt. Herbert L. Greer as a young man, and then we hear from him again, 60 years later, as he talks with the authors. In this way the tantalizing glimpse given by his wartime diaries comes to life as Herb provides the reader with a fascinating narrative of what life was like on Guam and aboard a B-29 during the firebombing of Japan in 1945.

Readers should note that there are some discrepancies between diary entries and historical fact. Mission dates are sometimes slightly out of sync depending on whether Herb was referencing the night he left on the mission or the next day when the bombing run actually took place. The number of aircraft he mentions that took part in a mission was usually based on numbers provided at the briefing sessions. Actual numbers were often lower due to aircraft readiness or re-deployment to other targets. In some cases Herb mentions hitting a target which is not listed in the many available mission chronologies. This is because the diary often refers to a specific target which Herb's squadron may have been assigned within the larger overall mission objective, or there may have been a target change.

Herb Greer, as a radio operator, saw life in a B-29 very differently from the pilot. No front row seat looking at the sky ahead, down at the sparkling ocean, or at Iwo Jima as they flew past at 20,000 thousand feet for our radioman. No chance to marvel at the sun as it peeks above the horizon, or as it slowly sinks to end another day. The radioman sits in a cramped space located around a blind corner, adjacent to the navigator, behind the upper gun turret; there are no windows. It's cramped and claustrophobic and the dangers all around are unseen. It reminds Herb of when he was a child and he couldn't see under his bed, but he just knew there was a bogeyman there. Unfortunately for Herb in 1945 the bogeymen were all too real, and he didn't wake up to find it was all just a dream.

The importance of a good crew and teamwork cannot be over-emphasized; it made the difference between surviving the inevitable tough times and not making it home.

It is interesting to note therefore that, after spending several months in close quarters, often during terrifyingly dangerous times, Herb didn't get to know the rest of his crew as well as you might think. You would expect that they would have discovered intimate details about each other – things that would bind them together, innermost thoughts and secrets that in other circumstances would never be told. At least, that's what your authors thought when interviewing Herb for this book. In fact, Herb didn't have a whole lot of information to impart. What was fascinating was that once he explained the situation we completely understood and it only served to accentuate what a unique time it was.

The crew of the City of Monroe was formed under expedited conditions, as were most crews at that time, the only thing they had in common initially was the desire to get overseas fly their 32 missions and come home. What was uncommon about this crew was that they were from all over the United States, Louisiana, Washington, New York, New Jersey, Illinois, Oklahoma and Texas. They were from small towns and large cities, Houston, Chicago, New York, Spokane and Monroe. Their families were farmers, movie stars, policemen, teachers, musicians, truck drivers and railroad workers. Some spoke with a southern twang, others had New York and Jersey accents, and the sounds of the Midwest and Northwest were represented as well. These guys really had nothing in common other than to fight this war with Japan.

Imagine you had to put your life in the hands of ten other men, but you couldn't choose who they would be, and to make matters worse you could only share one thing in common with them. What would you choose as that common trait?

Herb couldn't choose, but if he had been able to he would probably have chosen the one thing that made the crew of the City of Monroe a team - that they all wanted to fight for the liberty and freedom of their country.

The view most of us have of wartime and the camaraderie of soldiers, seamen and flyers comes from the romanticized version we are fed by Hollywood and television. In reality, for Herb, there was little time for idle chatter; flying a B-29 was no easy task. Each member of the crew had a serious job to do and losing concentration meant losing lives. When they were on a mission there was not a whole lot of time to talk. Fear dries mouths and talking about home only made them miss it more. Back at base our fearless flyers were too tired to relive the mission, or discuss much else. During the months Herb was in Guam the missions came hard and fast, so free time was valuable and invariably spent eating and sleeping.

As you read through the diaries you will meet some of the characters that made up the crew of the "The Reluctant Dragon" and "The City of Monroe." Others will remain as shadowy ghosts carrying out their missions from inside the giant hulk of the aircraft; crew members that Herb often never saw during a mission; their voices, mixed with static, the only thing that made them real–that and the fact that his life depended on them.

ON OUR
WAY
(APRIL 1945)

─── CHAPTER FIVE ───

A mysterious bond of brotherhood makes all men one.
– Thomas Carlyle

17,492 tons of bombs dropped

13,209 tons High Explosive; 4,283 tons Incendiary

3,487 sorties, 3,246 effective[2]

APRIL 1945
We left the states one
evening 12:00 I had been
visiting with the folks till
9:45 I had to leave to go
to 10:00 PM Briefing for the
hop, we went to the plane
from briefing and took off
from Mathew at midnite
We crossed frisco about 10

---

[2] http://www.ww2guide.com/b29ops.shtml

NEWS

The war in Europe was in its final stages in April, 1945. U. S. troops poured over the Rhine by the thousands—in boats, over bridges, through the air. Now even the most professionally pessimistic observers had to admit that the final round was on. The roads to Berlin had opened up.

At home, the average American took this significant advance in his stride. A year ago, such a tremendous push might have started public celebrations. By now, the U.S. people, like their Army, had become more professional in their attitude toward war. They were also, as ever, mindful of the cost.

In the week before the Big Push, U.S. casualties reached an all time high—19,998 for seven days. Over 850,000 Americans had been injured or killed in the war to date, more than twice those in World War 1. And the battlefront pictures showed the cemeteries growing ever larger[3].

A Japanese broadcaster reporting on the B-29 raids during the last half of March was quoted in Time magazine as saying "Red fire clouds kept creeping high and the tower of the Parliament Building stuck out black against the background of the red sky. During the night we thought the whole of Tokyo had been reduced to ashes." The combined effect of thousands of B-29's and M-69 incendiary bombs was proving lethal.

Early in April the Japanese took a massive hit to both their Air Force and their navy, losing more than 400 planes and several ships, including their prized battleship the Yamato, in a failed attempt off Okinawa to catch the U.S. navy by surprise.

President Franklin Roosevelt died on April 12 from a cerebral hemorrhage. The announcement was made by the White House at 5:48 p.m. and it was broadcast, over the radio, to the nation minutes later.

Amazingly, the Japanese publicly offered their condolences to the American people, proving once more the difficulty in understanding this enemy nation's culture. It is hard to imagine the Nazis in Germany giving a second thought to the death of the U.S. president, except perhaps to celebrate!

Stateside, at the movie theater, Herb's family would have been watching 'Without Love', a comedy romance, starring Katharine Hepburn and

[3] Time Magazine April 2, 1945

Spencer Tracy and 'Murder My Sweet', a Raymond Chandler, Philip Marlowe mystery starring Dick Powell and Claire Trevor.

April, 1945

We left the states one evening at 12 o'clock midnight. I had been visiting with the folks 'til 9:45 PM. That evening I had to leave to go to attend a 10:00 PM briefing for the hop. We went to the plane from briefing and took off from Mather Army Air Force Base at midnight. We crossed Frisco about ten minutes later and headed out to sea on course. We flew until 9:00 am that morning and landed at John Rodgers field in Oahu T.H. I met some of my old friends there; we took off the 2nd day on the second leg of our hop and 7 hours later landed at Kwajalein in the Marshall Islands. We had to remain there for an extra day due to trouble with # 3 engine. It had a broken push rod, which ruined # 5 cylinder. The next day we took off on the third leg of our hop and landed six hours later on Saipan in the Marianas, which I thought was our destination. But they (the Wing Commander) took our ship, so we laid over a day. The next afternoon they sent us down to the OATC (Oceanic Air Transport Command) terminal where we boarded a C-46 transport and were flown to Guam where we were permanently stationed. We have been here for about three days, and they assigned us a B-29 yesterday. We haven't flown it yet, but I imagine we will be over the target before long! The food is good here, but the bathing and washing facilities aren't so hot. We are washing out of our helmets and showering under barrels. Incidentally, there are still about 1,500 Japs loose on this island.

Unlike later enteries, Herb's Diary at this point, takes us from the time he leaves the U.S. to when he arrives at Guam. Fortunately, we have Herb 60 years later to fill in the blanks.

I remember the day I said goodbye to Mom and Dad as if it were yesterday. It was 20 April, 1945 and I was in Sacramento, California at Mather U.S. Army Air Corp Base. It was real good to catch up with all the news from back home before heading off. Although we were all putting on a brave face it was getting time for me to leave again and this time it wouldn't just be for

training; game time was quickly approaching. I had to say goodbye at about 9:45pm as I had to attend a briefing for the hop. It was to be our first combat destination, but none of the crew knew at this stage where we would end up.

The briefing pretty much went off as normal and we were also told what to do upon arrival at our destination. The radio operators were told when, where and who to make contact with and given all the codes and "challenges" we would need to identify ourselves. That, along with the operating frequency and the timing of the reports, just about gave us what we needed. We had to prepare for whatever might happen, both the likely and the totally unexpected. Radio operators met together at a specialized briefing, as did pilots, navigators and bombardiers, as we all had to concentrate on our own specific role if we, as a crew, were to function effectively in a crisis. The critical part of my job was the accuracy and timeliness of my reports, not only for our aircraft, but also for all the others in our formation or group.

After the briefing we walked to our plane. It was a cool night and as I looked up I saw stars appearing and disappearing between scudding clouds. It was just after midnight when we crossed San Francisco and headed out to sea. I used the time as we flew to try to keep up to date with my diary writing, snatching a few minutes sleep here and there on my Army Air Corps radio table, compliments of my Uncle "Sam."

One of the reasons I kept the diary was that it kept me awake. Just sitting there waiting for something to happen was mind-numbingly boring and you started to think about the mission and what might happen to you. It didn't do to think too much like that.

It was at this moment that it dawned on me with incredible clarity that this first leg of my journey to war placed me in the center of something that was so much greater than me. I was an important, but at the same time minute part of a war where hundreds of thousands of people were dying almost daily. This was history in the making and people would one day look back and judge what we were about to do – for better or for worse. Looking back, I think what I find intriguing is that, at 23 years of age, I could not begin to comprehend the magnitude of what I was getting into, or what my participation might mean.

I was excited, but scared and couldn't help wondering what my future held. Of course, at 23, I felt that all life was an adventure and like all young people had little sense of my own mortality. I guess that's why they send young men to war – ignorance truly is bliss.

We had been told to contact KSF Frisco, which is radio language for Alameda Air Station, California. We were to use a specific frequency within an hour of passing the Farallon Islands. At last, here was an opportunity to put into use all that I had learned in training and what I had taught to so many trainee radio operators.

The Farallon Islands, twenty-eight miles due west of the Golden Gate Bridge, are a group of craggy, wild rocks with quite a history. They used to be frequented by Russian sealers and their Aleutian female slaves. Not that I knew that in 1945. Of course in those days we didn't have the Internet, so it's been interesting over the last few years, to be able to research some of the places I used to fly over.

Whenever I flew I was always concerned about the radio failing. You never knew when a transmitter or receiver might malfunction. Returning to base for repairs was something none of the crew wanted; at that stage we all just wanted to get on with things!

In actual fact, that trip went without a hitch. I managed to contact KSF Frisco every hour with no problem. I remember thinking that this was a good omen.

We weren't the only ones leaving Mather that night. There were four or five planes leaving at timed intervals behind us. That was one of the reasons I radioed a report, encoded of course, that included our position and the weather we were experiencing all the way over the Pacific, at least until we reached our next reporting stage in the Hawaiian Islands. Once we reached those islands, Major Jones contacted Maui traffic control, by voice, for landing instructions. We had gotten the same information from the planes that were ahead of us, but it was a good feeling to think that we were all looking out for each other, part of a team, part of a bigger picture.

As we got closer to the action, we needed all the help we could get.

We arrived at John Rodgers Field in Oahu, Hawaii at 9:00am on 21 April, 1945 and later that morning I bumped into an old girlfriend from when I used to live in Grand Coulee – boy I was sure surprised to see her. Her name was Shirley Orgill; she had been on Oahu for about six months and was working as a secretary in the civil service. We chatted in a waiting room at the main gate about the islands and her new job; reminisced about the good times we had together and talked about where I might be going. As with so many chance meetings it was coincidence, but one that was never repeated, as I never saw or heard from her again.

I was with some of the crew later that evening when we walked past a movie theater and noticed a movie poster featuring Gene Autry. Well, our bombardier, who was a movie star himself when not fighting the Japanese, had a thing about Mr. Autry; there was a great deal of professional competition between the two, with Autry usually getting the better of Tim in the movie world. Tim's father Jack Holt had been in the movies for a number of years. Tim had been in "Stagecoach" with John Wayne, "My Darling Clementine" and numerous other movies such as "Treasures of Sierra Madre" with Humphrey Bogart and John Huston. By the time I got to know him, Tim had traded his horse and six guns, with bone handle grips, for a B-29 and a Norden bombsite. So we took the poster back to camp with us and the next day placed it over the bombsite, right next to where Tim sat. The air of expectancy was high and everyone was silent, and trying not to laugh, as he climbed into the aircraft. We didn't have to wait long before it became obvious that he had found the offending image – his use of the English language took on inspired new heights, to include some words that even we didn't recognize.

At the peak of his career in the 1940's "B" westerns, Tim Holt was the "fastest draw" in the movies with the ability to draw his revolver in five frames of film (slightly over one-sixth of a second).

The next day we were off again on the second leg of our hop heading for Kwajalein in the Marshall Islands, about 2,100 miles southwest of Hawaii and 1,400 miles east of Guam.

That was some trip! About fifty miles out from Kwajalein, Major Luther Jones, our Aircraft Commander, called me over the interphone; there was trouble with the number three engine and he was having difficulty keeping the aircraft stable and on course. I had just been thinking about a good meal and perhaps a cool beer and here he was asking me to crawl into the tunnel and take a look at the propeller for number three engine.

This meant I had to get up into the crawl-way and look out the astrodome, which is a Plexiglas bubble located on the top of the aircraft behind the upper forward turret Once there I observed that the propeller was swaying back and forth by four to five inches. As you can imagine this was not good. As soon as I relayed this information to Major Jones, he slowly shut down number three engine and feathered it. We finished the flight safely on three engines, thankful that this was not a combat mission.

It was sure nice to know that we had four engines and that this monster bird could fly pretty well on just three. However when I was in Alamogordo, in 1944, I learned the hard way that two engines lost on the same side was a very serious problem, especially during take off. I was training radio operators at the time, and during take off we lost two engines on the same side; this meant we never really achieved controlled flight (referred to as the 'step') and ended up plowing a local field a mile or two away. We came down pretty hard and the aircraft caught fire; we escaped but the aircraft was totally burned to the ground.

It was comforting to know that I was part of a highly experienced crew that had considerably more airtime than most other crews. Every one of the eleven-man crew was an expert. This gave me a great sense of security.

We spent the night in Kwajalein. There wasn't much to do so we pretty much just slept, ate and drank. Later the next day we were briefed on the next leg of our hop and discovered that we were heading to Saipan in the Marinaras.

It turned out that our number three engine had a broken push rod which completely shot the number five cylinder, so we ended up hanging around in Kwajalein while they repaired it.

Myself and some of the crew went down to the beach and watched with interest as some maintenance personnel pushed two B-25 Mitchells off into the ocean with a bulldozer. It looked like both aircraft had served their time well and were definitely war weary and unsafe to fly. They had removed any salvageable parts for use on other aircraft.

At Kwajalein, they roped off our B-29 and placed a sign, "Warning Classified Do Not Enter," at the perimeter. At that time the B-29 was still somewhat of a secret and boasted a lot of state-of-the-art equipment. What was humorous was that a B-24 crew, in response to this, had made their own sign for their aircraft which read "B-24 Liberator, everyone is welcome to look at it." I personally did not take them up on their offer since I had seen and flown in a number of them in the past.

On a more chilling note we saw two large mounds of earth approximately 25 feet wide and 150 feet long which hid large trenches filled with dead Japanese soldiers –casualties of the American invasion.

Later that day, lounging on the beach, I saw what appeared to be three Navy cooks drag two, five-man life rafts which they had tied together, down to the beach and launch them into the lagoon. They then tossed hand grenades into the water some distance away. After five grenades had exploded they paddled to the site of the explosions and proceeded to fill the empty raft with huge amounts of fish of all kinds. They say that creativity is the mother of invention; well these guys certainly invented a new and very effective way to fish!

The crew and I found this quite funny. Later that evening we noticed that the fish had made it onto the menu along with the traditional 'navy beans.'

It was these sorts of interludes that kept us real and gave us a few hours respite from thinking about what was going to happen to us when we got into the thick of things.

On 23 April at 10:00am we boarded our newly repaired B-29 and took off for Saipan. It took us six hours and we had to coax the aircraft every bit of the way. We ended up naming it "The Reluctant Dragon" because we had to cross the International Date Line on the journey and the aircraft really didn't seem to want to make the effort.

I still have the certificate we were awarded for crossing the 180th meridian and it is inscribed with the words:

DOMAIN OF THE GOLDEN DRAGON
RULER OF THE 180TH MERIDIAN

"To all sailors, soldiers, marines, wherever ye may be and to all mermaids, flying dragons, spirits of the deep, devil chasers and all other living creatures of the yellow seas, GREETINGS: Know ye that on this 24th day of April 1945 in latitude 12° 05" longitude 180° there appeared within the limits of my august dwelling the "The Reluctant Dragon" (B29-46-9913). Hearken ye, the said vessel, officers and crew have been inspected and passed on by my august body and staff. And know ye: Ye that are chit signers, squaw men, opium smokers, ice men and all round landlubbers that S/Sgt H.L. Greer having been found sane and worthy to be a dweller of the Far East has been gathered in my fold and duly initiated into the Silent Mysteries of the Far East. Be it further understood: That by virtue of the power vested in me I do hereby command all money lenders, wine sellers, cabaret owners, hotel managers and all my other subjects to show honor and respect to all his wishes whenever he may enter my realm. Disobey this command under penalty of my august displeasure.

Golden Dragon – Ruler of the 180th Meridian.

There was always a great deal of humor to relieve the tension, and I know that I, for one, was grateful for it.

Almost as soon as we arrived in Saipan the Wing Commander took the Reluctant Dragon away from us and gave it to another crew. I can't say we were unhappy to see it leave.

I had first thought that Saipan was to be our final destination, but was later informed that our last hop was to be to Guam.

All this traveling, and on Uncle Sam's dollar! At the time I thought how lucky I was to be seeing all these countries and having all these experiences. It was not until later that I discovered just how much the experience of a lifetime it would be.

We didn't have much chance to feel homesick or dwell for too long on concerns about friends and family back home. There was constant work to be done and much of it very demanding.

The crew said a not so fond farewell to the Reluctant Dragon, gathered together all our gear, personal effects and equipment and were sent down to the OATC (Oceanic Air Transport Command) terminal where we all boarded a C-46 transport aircraft and flew to Guam, where we were to be permanently stationed.

Over the next few days the crew got a little low; we had to wait for a new airplane and were told it could be a week before a crew arrived with one. It was unsettling being in a strange place and not knowing what lay ahead.

We all seemed to come back to life once we were assigned to the 62nd squadron, 39th Bomb Group. It made us feel that we belonged, as if we were part of a family. Guam's living quarters were surrounded by palm trees and at a different time, and under different circumstances we might have thought of this as exotic. Living in Quonset huts brought us down to earth; they were pretty basic, although some of the guys that had been in Guam for a while had spruced them up a little. Some of the huts had small gardens with banana plants and flowers grown from seeds that their loved ones had sent from home. Little touches like this were important to many people as they normalized an otherwise scary and stressful existence. At least we weren't in tents, which many before us had suffered. The Quonset huts weren't only used for accommodation. Dozens of them had been strung together to form a 54,000 sq. ft. warehouse – it was quite an impressive sight. It wasn't until years later that I discovered the name Quonset came from the Rhode Island town that made the huts.

Guam is about thirty miles long and was originally the home of the Chamorro Indians. Although the Americans had controlled the island for many years the Japanese took it over within three days of attacking Pearl Harbor. By August, 1944, though, the U.S. had taken back control.

Back in February 1945 bulldozers were still clearing the spot where the 39th Bomb Group would later have its operational base. Before that it was simply dense jungle. At that time only one runway was operational and the 19th and 29th Bomb Groups had already flown missions to Japan.

One scary thing I remember about those early days in Guam was that there were still around 1,500 Japanese wandering around in the jungle. It was rumored that they would creep up to the edge of the woods behind the outdoor theater area and watch the GI movies. Sometimes we heard rifle or machine gun fire and imagined our friends in the Marines reducing the enemy population. Those that had been there a while got used to the fact the enemy was out there prowling around, but I, like many of my comrades, slept with a military issued .45 automatic at the ready! And that just added to the uncertainty we all felt at that time. We were always on edge, waiting for something to happen.

I look back on those days and think to myself that Guam must be a great place to vacation now with its swaying palm trees, white sand beaches and jungle waterfalls, but to us, all those years ago, preparing for our war to start, it was an eerie place to wait. I would have preferred to see it all on a postcard rather than in person. The weather, when I was there, was unrelentingly hot and the conditions miserable.

No one ever asked me, but why couldn't we have had this crazy war somewhere less hot and humid, like the Bahamas perhaps? At least somewhere the mosquito wasn't considered the national bird!

There we were, young men waiting for the order to go into battle, to put our lives at risk and to use our new weapon, the massive and powerful B-29, to wreak destruction on the enemy. Emotionally, I am surprised we all managed to cope as well as we did. I suppose the young always feel immortal but there was always plenty of evidence to the contrary.

After three days on Guam, we were assigned a new B-29. The crew's anticipation was high and we couldn't wait to get her airborne. We all prayed that we had drawn a good aircraft and not another Reluctant Dragon.

To us, our ship was not an inanimate object; it became part of us, one of the team. Each crew member had his own relationship with the aircraft, and together we treated it much like you might a loved one. Something so important to your well-being that it becomes a part of your life, something you put trust in, something you look after and nurture, something you respect. The B-29 Superfortress is a huge structure, an aircraft giant, yet to a man we treated our new plane as if it had feelings and could understand us through the way we handled her. We patted her before we took off and thanked her when she returned us safely home. She was a pretty babe and we would be true to her through thick and thin, and somehow we knew she would be true to us.

Someone once said that the only difference between men and boys is the size of their toys, well that was pretty much us with our new B-29 and as soon as we could we gave her a name. We would call her "The City of Monroe" in honor of our Aircraft Commander Major Luther Jones' hometown.

The city of Monroe is in Louisiana, and is located along the Quachita River, which was singled out by National Geographic as one of the most beautiful in the world. It is a small and friendly place, and the birthplace of Delta Airlines. Near Monroe, at Poverty Point, is the site of North America's oldest human dwelling site. The region is a sportsman's paradise and enjoys a warm climate. Luther called Monroe home but he was born in Epps, Louisiana on December 7, 1917. His family moved to Monroe a few weeks before his sixth birthday.

Although we were all eager to get into the action, it was sobering to see planes returning from missions, with hundreds of holes, feathered engines and sundry mechanical problems. Of course, in many cases they were the lucky ones – we tried not to think about all those that didn't return at all.

We ran a pre-flight on our new plane and went over her with a fine-toothed comb to make sure everything on the aircraft was working properly. These were anxious times for the crew, but we needn't have worried, because as soon as we flew her we knew for certain she was no Reluctant Dragon. Having a plane that you can trust does a lot for your morale.

Over the next few days we settled into a routine and were kept busy preparing our new aircraft. Our squadron, the 62nd, had twelve aircraft, each with an eleven man crew, plus the ground and maintenance crews. We were proud to be part of it.

A Taste of War
(May 1945)

CHAPTER SIX

Fight the good fight of Faith. – 1 Tim. VI: 12.

24,285 tons of bombs dropped

6,937 tons High Explosive; 17,348 tons Incendiary

4,562 sorties, 4,226 effective[4]

> May 4 - 45
> We took our ship up today
> with 12 500 lb bombs and
> bomb an airstrip on a little
> Jap ocupied Island called
> Rota the mission was
> very successful we bombed
>
> Let it be your pride to show all men everywhere not only what good
> soldiers you are, but also what good men you are.—*Woodrow Wilson*

---

[4] http://www.ww2guide.com/b29ops.shtml

News

United States troops are still fighting the remaining Japanese on Iwo Jima, and they seize several islands off the coast of Okinawa. Nearly seven thousand US military personnel have been killed on Iwo Jima and there are 20,000 Japanese fatalities. It is interesting to note that only 216 Japanese were captured, reaffirming the fanatical mindset of the Japanese to fight to the death.

In Europe, the German forces are starting to surrender and by the end of the first week of May, all enemy forces in Northwest Germany, Holland and Denmark have surrendered. The US third, seventh and ninth armies are supporting British troops.

Amsterdam is liberated and a few days later General Jodl signs Germany's unconditional surrender. All fighting is scheduled to stop at one minute after midnight on 8 May, 1945.

Time magazine's cover for 7 May, 1945 showed a picture of Hitler with a red cross painted through it. There was no need for a headline.

Back at home the movies showing in May, 1945 included 'Molly and Me,' a comedy/musical starring Gracie Fields and Monty Wooley; 'It's in the Bag,' a comedy with Fred Allen, Jack Benny and Robert Benchley; and a romantic drama called, 'The Clock' about a soldier's two-day leave in New York, starring Judy Garland.

3 May, 1945

As Herb was getting ready for his first combat mission, 59 B-29's bombed airfields in Tachuarai, Miyazaki, Miyakonojo, Kokubu and Kanoya. Several other targets of opportunity were hit, 10 enemy fighters were downed and a single B-29 was lost. On another mission 88 B-29's mined Shimonoseki Strait and the inland sea; one didn't return.

4 May, 1945

On this day 21st Bomber Command missions 140 through 143 were carried out and 47 B-29's attacked airfields in Oita, Omura, Saeki and Matsuyama on Hyushi and Shikoku islands. One B-29 was lost.

May 4, '45. We took our ship up today with twelve 500-pound bombs and bombed an airstrip on a little Jap-occupied island called Rota. The mission was very successful. We bombed from 8,000 feet and dropped them in train. The 12 bombs went in a straight line down the center of the airstrip...and then we tried to swing the compass, but it was too cloudy and we returned to the base. When we landed we found a hole in the top of the rocker box cover on the number five cylinder for the number three engine. We were scheduled to make 5 night landings tonight, but the ship was out of commission. B-29's from here hit Kyushu airstrip, nine of them had landed at Iwo Jima because they were shot up and one ship landed at Iwo with the engineer dead.

May 4 was a training mission, very much like those we had completed in the States many times before, except of course for the live bombs. It was during these training missions that our crew learned to truly function as a team.

Rota was used by B-29 aircrews, during the initial Saipan/Tinian invasions, for target practice to train new bomber crews. Later, any B-29 with a breakdown that forced early return from a mission, would impale their bombs on the island prior to landing on Guam. Finally, of course, American aircrews would periodically strike the island just to keep the Japanese forces there from being able to harass US Forces on the other islands. I later learned that Rota was given the dubious distinction of being the single most bombed island during the Pacific War.

Swinging the compass meant comparing the true bearing to the compass reading. Navigators did this because the compass could be affected by the aircraft itself. Using an astro-compass, they would determine their true bearing using the sun. Once they knew their exact geographical coordinates and time of day, they could then compare this to the aircraft's compass reading and make the necessary corrections. If there were no problems they wouldn't need to check it for a couple of months, although if an engine was replaced for any reason, the whole operation would need to be done again.

During the flight we had trouble with number three engine – again. A push rod had come loose and hit the top of the rocker box, which covers the cams that operate the valves. This is at the top of the cylinder, so when that happened we started losing oil. You could see the brown streaks of oil blown back over the wing. We didn't have a maintenance person on board so upon landing our crew chief Marvin Rodich investigated. He removed the cowling and saw immediately that we had a broken rocker box.

Our crew chief and the Aircraft Commander checked for any equipment failures or any mechanical problem each time we landed and were responsible for clearing all repairs before we could get airborne again. The B-29's were a great airplane but some of them came straight from the factory into combat with little or no testing. No wonder bits and pieces kept falling off!

We were scheduled to make 5 night landings that night, but were unable to carry them out as our aircraft was being worked on by the ground crew.

B-29's from Guam hit Kyushu airstrip, but on the way back nine of them had to land at Iwo Jima because they were shot up and one ship landed at Iwo with the engineer dead.

As they were part of our group, we heard the details from the crews in the barracks and mess hall. I saw the plane in which the engineer died and it was already having its tail section replaced. You could always tell how rough a mission had been by the condition of the aircraft - that and the empty bunks.

It was this sort of thing that made you think about your future, although we tried hard not to dwell on it for too long.

A good crew chief could be a lifesaver when mechanical problems occurred, and Marvin was one of the best, with extensive experience on a wide range of aircraft. He was born in Ely, Minnesota quite close to the Canadian border and got his first airplane ride by cleaning oil from the windshield of a barnstormer who was selling rides. It is interesting to note that Herb's first flight was also with a barnstormer. Marvin got his first job as an airplane mechanic at the age of nineteen with Stebbins Aviation. He later became a licensed airframe and aircraft engine mechanic.

As the war approached he went to work for Mid-Continent Airlines at Minneapolis Airport. It was there he worked on Army Air Force P-51 Mustangs and on installing the extra fuel tanks on the B-25s which Dolittle used for his famous raid on Tokyo. Before flying on B-29's he was a Flight Engineer Crew Chief on Martin B-26's, towing targets over the Gulf of Mexico. It was this airplane that was nicknamed 'the Prostitute'; that is 'no visible means of support'. It was also known as 'The Widowmaker', although once pilots learned not to be afraid of its characteristics, it turned out to have the lowest loss rate in Europe.

It was Marvin and his team that kept Herb and the rest of the crew of the City of Monroe flying. He was quite a character and could always be relied on to have an inventory of '"misplaced supplies"' such as milk, food and beer. This stash was stored behind a secret wall at the back of the storehouse for the airman and officer's clubs.

Rodich was quite the inventor and built a scooter to travel around Guam. It was built using a small engine from a gas pump, the tail wheels from a Mustang and various other bits of scrap iron.

> *Marvin's ingenuity and skill with engines kept us a whole lot safer in the air than we might have otherwise been. We were very lucky to have him.*

5 May, 1945

On May 5, B-29's flew seven missions and bombed airfields in Oita, Tachiarai, Kanoya, and Chiran on Kyushu Island. A naval aircraft factory and arsenal were also hit at Kure; during this mission eleven Japanese fighters were downed and five B-29's were lost. The last mission on this busy day involved 86 B-29's dropping mines in Tokyo Bay, Ise Bay and at various points in the inland sea.

> *I suppose Guam wasn't too bad a place to be, but the bathing and washing facilities weren't so hot. We were washing out of our helmets and showering under barrels. Our uniforms were always dirty, as there were no laundry facilities. It was fun, not a whole lot of fun mind you, but then I suppose war isn't meant to be.*

> *We slept under mosquito netting at night, as the bugs were pretty bad. Trying to sleep in the day was pretty much impossible as the heat and*

humidity were too high and we didn't have the luxury of even a fan, let alone air conditioning.

The food wasn't bad though, which surprised us all. We actually got to eat real eggs, not the powdered version. The mess hall served fresh hot cooked food and we got breakfast, lunch and supper, if of course, we were there to eat it! It was huge and the entire 62nd Squadron could have eaten at the same time; that's twelve aircraft each with an eleven-man crew plus ground and maintenance crews.

One thing I really liked was that officers and enlisted men ate together, although some of the support groups such as bomb loaders had their own facility.

On May 7th Germany unconditionally surrenders. Victory in Europe is declared on May 8th and the allies celebrate. Just a few days earlier Herb had flown his first training mission off Guam, to Rota Island, in the northern Mariana Islands.

In these days of sophisticated communication where newspapers, television and radio provide immediate and graphic details of important events, it seems strange to look back and remember how we found out that our fellow flyboys had been lost or killed in action. It was far more subtle, but it affected us more, in a deeper, personal way. We found out in a piecemeal fashion. Familiar faces were not around at chow time and there were empty bunks that previously had living, breathing human beings in them. I am sure I was not alone in thinking that it could be my face missing at breakfast tomorrow.

7 May, 1945

A busy day where 41 B-29's bomb airfields at Oita, Ibusuki, and Kanoya on Kyushu Island. Allied forces destroy 34 Japanese aircraft and three B-29's are lost.

8 May, 1945

May 8: another mission over Rota, today dropped 2 500-lb bombs by radar in 6-ship formation in which we were the lead ship. Still haven't got a crack at Tojo's palaces. I wish they would let us go back to the states or fly some real bombing missions, I am getting tired of flying around this damn island of Guam with one wheel on the ground.

B-29's from Guam bomb airfields at Kanoya, Miyakonojo, Ōita, and Matsuyama on Kyushu and Shikoku Islands, Japan.

On 8 May, 1945 we flew back to Rota Island and practiced flying in formation with five other aircraft. We were the lead ship. Our radar operator, Lt. Landregan, got a chance to use his radar equipment. He was able to make any corrections it needed and then actually put a couple of bombs on target. It was exciting being lead ship as once our bomb bay doors opened so did those on the rest of the formation. A simple thing, but the effect was surprisingly profound.

I remember, in those early days on Guam, we were all getting frustrated. We wanted to fly some real missions over Japan, have a crack at Tojo's palaces, although in actual fact we were not allowed to bomb the imperial palaces.

The whole crew was going stir-crazy and I was sick of flying all around the damn island of Guam. Although we all knew we were safer carrying out training missions, the anticipation of the real action was weighing heavily on us.

We had to do 32 missions before we could go home and the two training missions over Rota didn't count, so that was another reason for us wanting to get on with things. We were young, full of reckless energy, with the patience of a long-tail cat in a room full of rocking chairs.

In my darker moments I used to wonder what the odds were of surviving one mission over Japan, let alone 32!

After we returned from Rota we found out that we'd lost three B-29's out of forty-one that bombed airfields at Oita, Ibusuki and Kanoya. So, I suppose that gave me some idea of the odds!

It was strange on 8 May to be celebrating V-E Day. The war in Europe was over, but my war had yet to begin. We heard that they were going to transfer experienced air, ground and naval forces to help us in the Pacific, but they never arrived. I suppose it was all over before they could get them reassigned.

10 May, 1945

10 May, 1945, Honshu. Our number 1 mission today, Jones, Holt, Landregen and Goldston sandbagged on this mission, but we all got credit for it. The Otake Oil Refinery was the target. And they plastered it with 500-pound bombs. There were reports there was smoke at 20,000 feet. Tim got a probable on a twin-engine Jap fighter and flak cracked the nose glass of our plane. Mission was very good, 400 B-29's participated in the raid.

May 10 was a busy day on Guam. Eight missions were flown and a total of 10 enemy aircraft were downed. One B-29 was lost. Once again airfields were hit along with a naval fuel station, coal yards, naval oil storage facilities and an oil refinery.

On 10, May 1945 we learned that we were to undertake our first combat mission, the first of our slated 32. I was excited and scared – in equal measures.

Our inaugural mission was actually #165 of the 21st Bomber Command in the Pacific War but for the crew of the "City of Monroe", our newly named B-29 – it was mission number one!

My first briefing session for a real combat mission was tense; we all realized that the stakes had just got a whole lot bigger. Briefings were a mixture of curiosity, excitement, fear and speculation with a healthy dose of tension added to the mix. It was the time you used to think about what might happen to you, and what, or who you were going to have to face. Basically, it was the fear of the unknown - none of us knew what to expect.

The briefings were by squadron, so we were one of twelve aircrews in the briefing room anxiously awaiting its start. The commander walked in quickly looking stern and stepped up onto the platform. As he took his seat he ordered us to sit down – some 142 of us. Everyone must have felt as tense as me because quickly the room became very quiet and sober.

The operations officer waited behind the podium while another officer stood to the right of a large wall map covered with drapes. It was an odd moment, akin to an opening ceremony.

It turned out that I was all hyped up for nothing as I soon discovered that I was not going to participate in our first mission. I, along with the six other members of the crew, were stood down so that Major Luther Jones, our Aircraft Commander, Tim Holt, the bombardier, Robert Landregan, the radar officer, and Marshall Goldston the flight engineer, could be supervised during the mission. Our guys were to be shadowed by a combat-seasoned crew who would offer help and advice during the flight. This was standard procedure and part of ongoing training.

The mission itself though was as real as it could be and was one of the most successful to date.

Although all our crew didn't go on the mission, we all got credit for it as part of the 32 we had to survive before going home. Every crew that took part received the Distinguished Unit Citation.

The mission Herb refers to was one of the most successful operations to date. During April the systematic job carried out by the 21st Bomber Command had curtailed the Japanese ability to produce aviation fuel. They were having to manufacture synthetic fuels and bring oil from outlying conquered countries. The fuel would be transported by vessel or aircraft and stored in the empire. The area around the Otake oil refinery was an important storage area for these products.

On May 19, an amazing 96% of bombs fell on target, and about 90% hit within 1000 feet of the aiming point. The official report showed that the Otake oil refinery plant was rendered completely inoperative and that 47% of it was destroyed outright.

Briefings were a serious matter and although there might be some joking around while waiting for the commander to enter the room, as soon as he did it was straight down to business. The operations officer would describe the mission, detailing what time the first aircraft would take-off and in what direction. Locations and routes were described and the second officer would point them out on the map. Further information would then be given by the intelligence officer who briefed the crew on the target. He would give the crews as much information as he could on the target including its general shape, size and location. Any information gained from reconnaissance photographs would be shared, including details on defenses, landmarks and the selected offset aiming points (OAP's). Once he was finished the communications, weather and engineering officers all took their turns in supplying further pieces of the puzzle.

Once the general briefing was over, the crews went to their specialized briefings, all the while asking themselves, and whoever else would listen, "Will this be the last mission?" "Will it all be over after this one?" For some it would indeed be their last mission.

If it was a night mission the crews would reassemble at 4:00pm. They would be issued their personal equipment of parachutes, side arms, flak helmets and vests, earphones and anything else they would need on the mission. This was no time for joking or fooling around; the crew were serious about the equipment that might save their lives.

It was then time to climb aboard the waiting trucks and be driven to the aircraft - gigantic birds beautifully majestic and uncharacteristically quiet – but not for long. The crew, standing on the steel and macadam hardstands, was dwarfed by these behemoths. The B-29 was 99 feet in length and almost 30 feet high. Its wingspan, at a staggering 141' 3", was almost half the length of a football field. Its like had never been seen before and it would wreak havoc on the enemy through its speed, power, and the enormous payload it could carry. One such beast was enough to elicit awe, but to see 500 in one place at one time, flying above you, targeting you, must have been like facing Armageddon.

This was a busy time for the crew; no time to think about what might happen; there would be plenty of time for introspection on the journey. The hardstands had an air of hundreds of worker bees fussing over their queen. Crews examined every inch of their aircraft during the pre-flight inspection, checking the bomber's fuselage, wings, tires, guns, propellers and everything else on the checklist. They all had a vested interest in ensuring everything was in order – the last thing anyone wanted was a surprise at 20,000 feet, especially over enemy territory.

> *Once the inspection was complete Major Luther Jones would line the crew up with all their equipment piled in front of them. He would move slowly along the line inspecting each piece of equipment to ensure it was combat ready. Once satisfied he would give us the order and we would don our Mae West life jackets and parachutes and begin loading everything onto our aircraft. Although a large aircraft, storing all the gear was no mean feat. While waiting for clearance we would often ask, "How about it Major, is this the last mission?" and he would answer, "It's the last one tonight!"*

> *As soon as the control tower cleared us for take-off, the atmosphere immediately turned tense. Getting one of these giants off the ground was not a foregone conclusion. As the City of Monroe rumbled off its assigned parking hardstand and taxied to its position on the runway, our anticipation grew. We became very quiet and were all praying. I never met an atheist on takeoff or over the target dropping bombs!*

A fully loaded B-29 trundling down the runway at Guam weighed in at 137,000 lbs. When you consider that this included some 20,000 lbs. of high explosives, 36,000 lbs. of fuel and 340 gallons of oil for the engines, you can understand the crew's apprehension.

> *As the plane taxied and then turned at the end of the runway Major Jones put on the bomber's brakes and ran the engines up to full power. The sound reverberated through the aircraft, everything shook as every ounce of this beast strained against its leash – and then, with a collective lump in every crew member's throat, the aircraft surged forward as takeoff power was applied and the brakes released. Four screaming engines gave their all, pulling this Goliath down the runway to its destiny, and ours. The next minute or so took a lifetime. We all knew that the runway was only so*

long and that at the end there was a cliff and beneath it a rocky beach – a graveyard for B-29's that didn't make it. At maximum weight it was always touch and go and we sat there waiting for the slight dip in the runway that marked the point of no return. Past that point we were committed to take off, whether we had reached sufficient air speed or not. As we left land we felt a drop as Major Jones would put her nose down slightly to give us some additional air-speed, aiding the engines which, pulling for all their worth, gradually re-established the momentary loss in altitude. We were on our way with a collective sigh of relief, and a return to our solitary thoughts. Those cliffs on Guam were an ally to those that made it and an enemy to those that didn't.

The journey was long and full of anxiety for the crew. As they got closer to their target they would be scanning the sky frantically looking for enemy fighters, their aircraft lighting up as anti-aircraft artillery fire burst in the air all around them.

It took between 30-45 minutes to reach our cruising altitude of 10,000 feet. Tim Holt would then come back from his bombardier station and together we would open the pressure door, and turn the lights on in the bomb bay. He would then go to the left of the bomb bay and I would go to the right and we would pull the tagged arming safety pins from the front and rear of each bomb. Depending on the type of bomb we were carrying there might only be one pin. While pulling the pins we would also check that the arming wires at each end of the bomb were inserted into the fuses. Although we were preparing the bombs there was no real danger as the fuses were only activated when the arming wires were pulled from the fuse as the bombs fell, allowing the propeller to spin a set number of revolutions as the bomb focused on its target.

Once finished we would leave the bomb bay and return to the pressurized cabin, turn the lights off and secure the pressure door. At this point we would count all the pins we had collected to make sure that we had pulled every one. At the same time we were doing all this, T/Sgt Tomlinson the CFC Gunner, and Lt. Landregan, the radar officer, would be doing the same thing in the rear bomb bay.

Back at my station, I would check that my transmitter and receiver were on and that the correct frequency was set. Opening my briefcase I would retrieve my codebooks and check the coding and decoding sections as they related to the code of the day. This allowed me to receive messages. However we were on radio silence, which meant we could not transmit for fear of enemy interception. Once I got all my chores done I'd plug in my hot cup, heat some coffee and grab a cigarette – just another day at the office! Actually, that about sums up the next six plus hours of monitoring the radio and trying to keep awake. There was no in-house movie or food service from attractive flight attendants to while away the hours, just memories and thoughts of my wife back home.

The radio had to be monitored continuously in case there was a change to our mission, or if I received a message from another aircraft in trouble. Periodically I would receive a message from base with an update on weather or a target change.

About an hour out from mainland Japan, Major Jones would notify the crew of the impending 'black tie' engagement we were about to 'gate-crash' as we began to prepare for action. This was the signal to align our flak curtains, put our flak jackets and helmets on in anticipation of hitting our IP (Initial Point) for the bombing run. What came next was the inevitable roller coaster ride as we went through the target area. In preparation, I would switch from my assigned frequency to the emergency distress frequency in case we got into trouble. During the bomb run the interphone was mute, the only sound was the drone of the engines, unless of course a shell exploded close to us. Some shells looked like black carnations bursting into bloom, like some sick horticultural joke.

During the time over the target the crew experienced a cold sweat of fear as they reached maximum exposure; then as they headed for the departure IP and left the mainland behind there was a noticeable lessening of anxiety, although with it came the awareness that "it's not over until the fat lady sings" and they were always more than ready to hear her break into song. Back out over open ocean the crew was tired, emotionally drained, but optimistic that they would survive another mission. Then the long flight home, 1500 miles and six to eight hours flying time to Guam, home such as it was. For Herb, staying awake was not the only issue – it was time to share his thoughts with his diary, once again.

Sixty years later he takes us back to his station onboard the City of Monroe as they head back out to sea, after dropping their bombs.

About 30 minutes later when we were 'feet wet' again, I would warm the coffee and light a cigarette, still checking both frequencies for any problems. It may sound like I was calm and collected, but in reality it was the most frightening experience you can possibly imagine.

As soon as we could make out Guam in the distance, we couldn't wait to get there. We were much like kids approaching a candy store!

When we landed, the trucks would meet us again and take us immediately to debriefing. Once again we would question whether this had been our last mission. Had the Japs had enough? Did they really want more of the same? Little did we know that we would ask this same question 25 more times before we finally got the answer we wanted to hear.

As we entered the debriefing room, weary from the journey, the anxiety and the emotional drain, there were chaplains to meet us and welcome us home. Our flight suits would be wet with sweat and stained as if we had been wearing them for weeks. At a debriefing table an intelligence specialist would question us about the mission, and no detail seemed to be too small or insignificant. It was dawn before we were finally allowed to leave the room, to a sky streaked with red toward the eastern horizon, to nature imitating what we had done to the skies over Japan.

As we walked slowly back to our quarters, other men were getting up to start work on preparing the giant Superfortresses for their next missions. Boy, were we tired and ready for bed! As we drifted off we thought to ourselves, how many beds will be empty in the morning – how many young men will be at permanent rest?

11 - 13 May, 1945

The crew of the City of Monroe didn't fly during this period but the action didn't stop, as 154 B-29's took part in bombing airfields at Saeki,

Oita, Nittagahara, Miyazaki and also Miyakonojo on Kyushu Island. The aircraft manufacturing plant at Kawanishi was also bombed and Shimonoseki Strait was mined.

Guam was busy as additional B-29's were arriving at Northwest Field from the United States.

14 May, 1945

1:00 AM May 14, 1945, Honshu. Our second bomber run hit Nagoya today, in a maximum effort raid. 550 B-29's participated in the raid. The hits were very good. This was a Mitsubishi aircraft factory. We hit the target yesterday at 19,500 feet with the 550 B-29's in separate elements. We were the lead ship in the third element to go over the target. We were carrying 24, 500-pound incendiary cluster bombs. "Smoke was observed at 19,000 feet, when we went over the target flak was moderate, not too heavy, although we received one small flak hole in our airplane. Two fighters were in the vicinity, but they did not attack us. One twin-engine Jap fighter went over us, about 5,000 feet above us, and Tommy peppered him with the six top guns and he left in a big hurry and stayed away from us. Return trip from the target was good.

In the early hours of May 14th, 472 B-29's bombed the northern part of Nagoya, an urban area. Some 20 Japanese fighters were claimed and 11 B-29's were lost, two over the mainland and nine between Nagoya and the Marianas, in the vast Pacific Ocean.

This was a big raid. Can you imagine almost 500 of these gigantic bombers attacking one town? I mention in the diary that we attacked in separate elements. Well each element had a specific objective within the overall target area. Four to five formations, made up of anywhere from five to seven aircraft, formed each element. As soon as the lead plane dropped its bombs, it was considered a "go" with regard to "bombs away" for the rest of the formation.

Flying a bombing mission is quite something! Rules and systems in this situation take on a whole new meaning. Everyone is responsible for a particular aspect of the mission and you have to rely on them to perform their duties to the highest level – your life depends on it!

Imagine, you are on a bombing mission, approaching the target. Your palms are hot and sweaty and the tension in the plane is palpable. Everyone has a job to do, and as we enter the target area, the responsibility for our lives and the success of the mission rests with our bombardier, Holt. It is he who will pilot us through this part of our mission to the designated target point, where we will drop several thousand pounds of thermite or jellied gasoline on Nagoya. It is he who will keep us on course and at the right altitude and speed, through shifting winds, heat and flak as the pilot mutely watches on.

Tim's bombsite is wired through the autopilot. For the next little while he will need all the concentration he can muster as he overrides it, and takes not only our lives in his hands but also the 100,000's of people below us that will soon feel the heavy hand of war upon them. He sights the target in the cross hairs of his indicator, the bomb doors open and he calls "bombs away!" and 12,000 lbs. of retribution rains down on the town below. In a split second the plane becomes lighter, unburdened of its heavy load, and Major Luther Jones reclaims control and we head for the withdrawal point.

By using this predetermined method, we minimized time over the target and the possibility of running into other flak batteries and aircraft, both friendly and unfriendly.

Five hundred planes dropping bombs sounds scary enough to frighten off the most dedicated enemy, but when you consider we were dropping 500-pound cluster bombs holding individual M-69 bombs containing jellied gasoline, fear takes on a whole new meaning. Our aircraft alone dropped 24, 500-pound cluster bombs on Nagoya that day. This gave a solid concentration of coverage and caused the fire to spread over a large area, burning through anything that was in its way. I think it is fair to say that the Japanese people were very aware that we had paid them a visit.

The cluster bomb broke apart 2,000 feet above its target, raining down M-69 jellied gasoline bombs in directed clusters. As the small tube-like bombs (3 inches in diameter and 20 inches long) fell, each ejected a cloth tail which caught in the wind, stabilized it, and controlled the speed of its descent. On impact the napalm ignited and shot some 100 feet out of the tail of the bomb in a burning jet, spraying jellied gasoline on anything in its way.

Napalm sets extremely hot fires which burn slowly and spread effectively. It is particularly good at burning wood and paper which were the primary construction materials used in building Japanese cities at the time.

 Not everyone on the ground died from the terrible burns these weapons inflicted. Many died from carbon monoxide poisoning caused by the massive de-oxygenation created by the fires. Being undercover may have been protection from the napalm itself but not from the lack of oxygen. Carbon monoxide paralyzes its victims, taking away their ability to think or move. It is interesting to note that the pre-cursor to bombs carrying napalm were the flame-throwers used in WWI.

In the Middle Ages when heretics were burnt at the stake, it was better to be atop a large fire than a small one. Those treated to the effect of a grand fire were dead of carbon monoxide poisoning a long time before they actually felt flames licking at their heels.

We were formally introduced to the Jet Stream today – before the war no one knew of its existence! We on the other hand got to be on a first-name basis with it. It could produce winds of up to 200 miles an hour. This meant our aircraft could be traveling at 250 mph indicated air speed while flying into a 200 mph headwind, and the ground speed would actually be 50 mph. If the aircraft was flying at 250 mph indicated air speed with a 200 mph tailwind, its gound speed would be 450 mph. This was the primary reason Gen. Curtis LeMay ordered us to fly at much lower altitudes, to allow for more concentrated bombing with greater accuracy.

I remember the 14th of May mission well. There was smoke coming up at us from the previous aircraft strikes and the flak was all around us. Then, there was a sudden thump and I knew we'd been hit – we were lucky – it was just a small hole near the wing. But, the updrafts of hot air from Nagoya burning below were causing smoke to rise, and with it burning embers of God knows what, were entering the bomb bay.

We were bouncing around like a toy plane attached to a string held by an inexperienced child, with the thermals jerking and tugging at us. Enemy flak and a firestorm beneath us, created by more than 500 bombers dropping some five million pounds of incendiaries, were also giving us trouble.

Then, as we dropped our load, the aircraft immediately became six tons lighter and although we were trimmed to fly level, we rose instantly, aided by the intense, hot air rising to greet us. Ordinarily this was not a problem, but we were in a theater of war with 499 other large aircraft, all crammed into a relatively small air space, and with limited visibility. Above us, somewhere, were other B-29's. As Major Jones fought to keep us level, we could only sit and hope we weren't going to get a whole lot more familiar with the other aircraft than we wanted. It wouldn't be the first time that two B-29's had ran into, or dropped bombs on each other. Unfortunately, this happened far too often, with the winds and thermals from the firestorm below tossing these aircraft around as if they were toys.

As we started to fly to the withdrawal point, we saw two Japanese fighters in the distance, but they didn't get close. Then at about 5,000 feet, a twin engine Jap fighter came out of nowhere and Tommy peppered him with the six top guns. He got out of there fast and never bothered us again. Our gunnery system was very sophisticated by the standards at that time; any gunnery position could take control of one or more remote gun turrets and fire simultaneously at oncoming aircraft. Not only that, the central control firing system would automatically calculate and compensate for wind and airspeed, which greatly improved our accuracy.

Our return trip gave me some additional time to write a few lines in my diary. After all the action there was an anti-climax and I found it difficult to stay awake. A radioman can't sleep though, not for a moment, it's our job to monitor the radio at all times before, during and after the raid, so I just battled through the rest of the trip. This was to become a familiar theme.

In the early days of our time over Japan we thought a lot about what we were doing and the effect we were having on people's lives. It was a sick feeling knowing you had destroyed lives, but what kept us going was the thought that these people wanted us dead and would settle for nothing less than to kill each and every non-Japanese they could.

In the same way Japanese leaders had dehumanized the enemy to their soldiers, so Herb and his crew dehumanized their enemy. The way they saw it, they were just doing their job, protecting their country. It was the only way these young men could cope with what they had to do.

Although the firebombing of Japan was highly successful, many men continued to lay down their lives for their country throughout the Pacific theatre and this particular day was destined to take its toll. One plane from the 462nd Bomb Group, shot down by Japanese fighters, was last seen circling, flaming and smoking and then crashing into Isewan Bay near Nagoya city. The crew? One man was killed in the action, seven were found guilty of indiscriminate bombing and were beheaded on 12 July, 1945 at Obatagahara rifle range just outside Nagoya and three ended up in Ofuna POW camp. Only two of the crew ever made it back to the US.

The fate of all the B-29's that crashed that day is not known, but the crew of a B-29 from the 19th Bomb Group met a similar fate as those from the 462nd; - seven were killed in action and the four survivors were captured, interrogated and later executed by beheading.

Another aircraft was hit by flak over Nagoya and caught fire. As it was descending, part of its wing came off and it plummeted to the ground. No parachutes were seen and the crew perished.

These young heroes were not easily deterred though, and through the mayhem, the flak, and the fighters, they continued to fly. History tells of one plane continuing on to the target with its number one engine lost; it then lost its number two engine and was forced to ditch. This crew fared better than many others and only lost two of their eleven crew members.

At the same time, an aircraft attempting to land with a feathered prop, crashed and burned, losing seven men and leaving 4 wounded.

Others lost engines or ran low or out of fuel and were forced to head for Iwo Jima, or ditch on their way in. Weather conditions were often severe around Iwo Jima and this meant crews, desperate for somewhere to put down, had nowhere to go. Their only option was to bail out into an angry sea. Most were saved, but many others were lost to the sea.

We talk about them being men but these were really boys doing a man's job; few were older than 25 and many were far younger. They would never forget what they saw and what they experienced as long as they lived. It would haunt many of them and alter their psyche to such an extent that they would never be the same again. Others would remain in the military with people who understood them, never leaving the comparative safety of this familiar environment, where the insanity of war was always just a step away but their lives still made sense. Being in the military meant they never completely left the war – they remained on permanent standby. It is as if being on a continual war footing kept the demons away.

17 May, 1945

May 17, 1945. Target: southern Nagoya, Nakajima aircraft factory. Hit Nagoya again at 3:00 AM this morning, was a night raid. One ship had the tail gunner dead when they got back. A flak shell burst close to him and practically blew off his head. Low level, we went in at 12,000 feet, very low flak was seen, although other ships ahead of us were hit badly. Raid was good and very big fires were observed over the target. We returned without mishap.

The bombing of Nagoya continued with a staggering 533 B-29's, dropping tens of thousands of pounds of high explosives onto the urban areas, specifically picking out the aircraft works, the arsenal and the Nippon Vehicle Company. Three B-29's were lost on this day.

The early aircraft on this run got hit with a lot of flak, but by the time we got to drop our load it had eased off a bit. One ship got hit pretty badly, the concussion thundering through the plane. As the plane managed to get to a lower altitude one of the crew went back to check on the gunner, who wasn't answering his interphone calls, but the flak shell had sent shrapnel tearing through the tail like shotgun pellets through a pheasant, practically blowing his head off.

We were lucky; the Japanese gunners didn't throw a whole lot at us. Maybe they had run out of ammunition or as the fires got closer to their ammunition supply, they simply ran off to seek shelter. Quite often their searchlights weren't working properly and that made us difficult to spot. That's not to say we didn't get some attention because we did see flak bursts of shrapnel all around us. We thought it might have been from German 88's, since Germany and Japan were allies and shared their military hardware.

The target for our 500-pound general-purpose high explosive bombs was the factory making "Betty bombers," the G4M, a twin-engine land-based bomber. This plane had enormous range and a good top speed. We sure were glad we weren't flying it though, as it was known as a firetrap. The wings were fuel tanks and there was no armor plating to protect the crew. I can only imagine how exposed the crew must have felt. The Betty was easy prey for the allied fighters and even easier for us B-29's who destroyed them before they even rolled out of the factory.

It was a big night for the 20th Air Force as some 194,000,000 square feet (6.97 square miles) of Nagoya were destroyed. That's 13.7% of the entire city. If we add that to the previous raids 345,000,000 square feet or 12.7 square miles, some 24.4% of the city had been destroyed.

19 May, 1945

May 19, 1945. Primary target Takasnnaki Army Arsenal. The secondary Hamamatsu propeller factory. Bomb mission number 4 hit the Jap mainland again today, but there was a heavy overcast and our radar was jammed. Bombing was not too effective as far as I know. The ground was absolutely obscured. The overcast reached to 26,000 feet and 10/10 coverage and we were briefed for 2/10 coverage. Our load was 20 each 500-pound general purpose bombs. Our flight time on mission was 14 hours. We bombed a secondary target. There were 500 ships.

Herb's spelling in his diary was a little awry at this point and the army arsenal he and his crew were targeting was actually in Tachikawa not Takasnnaki. Tachikawa is on east central Honshu Island in the central part of the Tokyo prefecture. The city is on the Tama River and lies about twenty miles west of downtown Tokyo. Nowadays it is an industrial center, manufacturing machinery and automobiles.

*Tachikawa was our fourth mission and by now we were getting used to
our aircraft and each other. We were with 21 other planes from our group,
the 39th, and were armed with general-purpose bombs, 20 of them at 500-
pounds apiece. That's a lot of hardware. These things will rip anything
apart, that's always assuming you hit something. It was a tough mission,
and not very successful. It was a radar run and we approached from the
land side, but the Japs jammed our radar and on top of this we couldn't see
our target through the cloud cover. We ended up going for our secondary
target, which was a propeller factory at Hamamatsu. Later we found
out that Hamamatsu was also home to the Japan Musical Instrument
Company. We were always given an alternate target, so whatever happened
we always had somewhere to drop our bombs.*

*The sky was heavy and overcast due to a Siberian cold front hitting the
warm Pacific air. We had to route around a lot of thunderheads and we
were being tossed, turned and bounced around. I felt like I was riding a
particularly unfriendly and explosive bull at a rodeo. It was a sobering
thought that I was straddling 10,000 pounds of high explosives!*

*Our bombardier, Tim Holt, wrote a parody about this mission, which
became famous within the 39th Bomb Group. It wasn't all that refined but
it summed up our feelings after having our radar jammed and having to fly
blind due to bad weather conditions.*

The verse that Herb refers to is:

There's a dream boat just leaving for Guam,

Bound for the empire to bomb,

This isn't the first time; they've been there before.

They know what they're going to do.

They did a burn job on old Tokyo,

One on Nagoya too.

They burned up Osaka and blew up Otake,

And f_ _ _ _ _ 'em up on Hamamatsu.

24 May, 1945

May 24, 1945, Honshu. Target, Tokyo industrial center in central part. 4,500 ton of incendiaries were dropped by all aircraft. Seen about half a dozen Baka planes over the target. Flak was moderate to medium heavy. There were quite a few searchlights in the Tokyo area, and as we left the area we had eight (Japanese) fighters follow us out from the mainland 250 miles out to sea. When we finally left them, mission was successful, fires could be seen 150 miles out to sea, 12 planes were lost.

In talking to Herb it became obvious that the distances in his diary entry of sixty years ago had been transposed. The Japanese fighters followed the City of Monroe 150 miles out to sea before they turned back and the fires from the city could be seen 250 miles out to sea.

This mission was an all-out attack on Tokyo – this time we really meant business and dropped an appalling amount of bombs on the city. The searchlights in Tokyo were lighting up the sky looking for us and the flak was fairly heavy; it was bursting all around us. It was clear that the Japanese had fortified the major cities, which housed military manufacturing plants.

As we passed through the target area, the plane was blacked out; it was totally dark save for the dull red glow coming from the instrument panels. Suddenly the most intense bright light flooded the aircraft, blinding us – the tension in the aircraft shot up, hearts started beating a whole lot faster as we instantly realized that we were being picked out of the sky by a searchlight and were now firmly in the sights of air and ground fire. From that moment everything went into slow motion as we passed through the target – seconds felt like minutes and minutes, hours. They say that you can taste fear – well they're absolutely right!

We managed to complete the mission and leave the target unscathed, but once heading out to sea we picked up eight enemy fighters. We were still blacked out and had they been able to see us they would have surely attempted to shoot us down or ram the aircraft in an attempt to destroy us. We could see the Jap pilot's silhouette in the canopy green house.

We were 150 miles out to sea and the fighters had turned toward home, having not seen us. Looking back we saw the inferno that was once Tokyo. It was burning brightly, sending smoke thousands of feet into the air – I imagined that this is what the end of the world would look like, and of course, for many it was.

Later, some 250 miles out to sea, the crew saw what looked like a most amazing sunset, at its center a large red fireball. Testimony to what some nine million pounds of bombs can do to match nature's fiery end to a day.

As the crew flew home the smell of burning human flesh permeated the aircraft, a sweet smell, but rancid – a constant reminder of man's inhumanity to man. Intelligent people had brought this destruction upon themselves and the City of Monroe must have seemed like one of the four horsemen of the apocalypse - the pale horse of death. The smell of death lingered all the way home and they took the burning flesh into their own bodies with each breath for the eight hours it took them to return to Guam. It was something that would stay with them forever.

Men, women and children on the ground were being turned into flaming torches, their clothes bursting into flames. They could be seen from the air running to bridges and throwing themselves into the water. This would not have saved them however, as the water in the rivers was boiling, so intense was the firestorm raining down on them.

It was hard to understand why the Japanese military would not admit defeat in the face of such overwhelming destruction, such massive loss of life. On 9 March, two months before Herb's first mission, the twentieth Air Force had attacked Tokyo with 334 B-29's. 84,000 people were killed, 41,000 were injured 250,000 buildings were destroyed and sixteen square miles of Tokyo were razed to the ground. And now they had just shown the enemy that they could destroy at will. The young crew would have been forgiven for asking, "what will it take to make them give up?"

Don and Herb Greer (L to R) in Washington

L to R- Herb, Shirley and Don Greer

Herb Greer (1938) working at Grand Coulee Dam as a jackhammer operator.

Dutch Harbor, AK 1940

Herb in cadets at Santa Ana

Newspaper article on the attack of Dutch Harbor in 1942.

DECK BUCKLED—S.S. Northwestern, station
... used as barracks for construction work-
... shown after it had been blasted by Jap

bombs in June 3-4 raids on Dutch Harbor.
Deck plates and one side section of the vessel's
... appears to be badly buckled. One

bomb smashed into a gangway entrance, apparently used for vehicle deliveries. Another
Dutch Harbor picture on Page 3.

Jean Greer in Salem, AR while Herb's overseas

Herb and Jean Greer married July 16, 1944

Herb prior to leaving for the Pacific

Living Quarters (Quonset Huts) on Guam

Local School in Guam

GI Outdoor Theatre on Guam

Local teachers on Guam

The native settlement of Agana

Native Guamanian at work

Native Guamanian at work

Local church in Agana damaged by invasion

Herb in a coconut palm on Guam. It's easier to climb up than climb down, because the bark points up.

Tim Holt in his Non-Military job

*Tim Holt's Military
Academy picture.*

*B-29s on taxiway
for takeoff*

L to R- Herb and Don Greer on Guam

*B-29 frontal
picture on
Guam*

Herb and Don Greer next to B-29 Jughaid on Guam

Herb's B-29 crash in Alamogordo

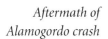

Aftermath of Alamogordo crash

*B-29's back on Guam
on hardstands*

*B-29 on taxiway next to
the cliffs on North Field*

*Ground crew and Don
Greer (3rd from right) in
front of "City of Monroe"*

Chaplain Services

Cover of the Government Issue Diary

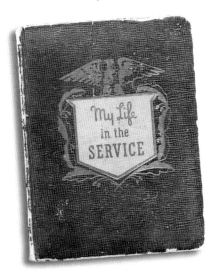

Dip in the runway (the point of no return) committed for take off

日本國民に告ぐ

TRANSLATION

READ THIS CAREFULLY AS IT MAY SAVE YOUR LIFE OR THE LIFE OF A RELATIVE OR FRIEND. IN THE NEXT FEW DAYS, THE MILITARY INSTALLATIONS IN FOUR OR MORE OF THE CITIES NAMED ON THE REVERSE SIDE OF THIS LEAFLET WILL BE DESTROYED BY AMERICAN BOMBS.

THESE CITIES CONTAIN MILITARY INSTALLATIONS AND WORKSHOPS OF FACTORIES WHICH PRODUCE MILITARY GOODS. WE ARE DETERMINED TO DESTROY ALL THE TOOLS OF THE MILITARY CLIQUE WHICH THEY ARE USING TO PROLONG THIS USELESS WAR. BUT, UNFORTUNATELY, BOMBS HAVE NO EYES, SO, IN ACCORDANCE WITH AMERICAN WELL-KNOWN HUMANITARIAN PRINCIPLES, THE AMERICAN AIR FORCE WHICH DOES NOT WISH TO INJURE INNOCENT PEOPLE, NOW GIVES YOU WARNING TO EVACUATE THE CITIES NAMED AND SAVE YOUR LIVES.

AMERICA IS NOT FIGHTING THE JAPANESE PEOPLE BUT IS FIGHTING THE MILITARY GROUP WHICH HAS ENSLAVED THE JAPANESE PEOPLE.

THE PEACE WHICH AMERICA WILL BRING WILL FREE THE PEOPLE FROM THE OPPRESSION OF THE MILITARY AND MEAN THE EMERGENCE OF A NEW AND BETTER JAPAN.

YOU CAN RESTORE PEACE BY DEMANDING NEW AND GOOD LEADERS WHO WILL END THE WAR.

WE CANNOT PROMISE THAT ONLY THESE CITIES WILL BE AMONG THOSE ATTACKED BUT AT LEAST FOUR WILL BE, SO, HEED THIS WARNING AND EVACUATE THESE CITIES.

The list of doomed cities printed on the opposite side of the leaflet are Aomori, Nishinomiya, Ogaki, Kurume, Ichinomiya, Nagaoka, Koriyama, Hakodate, Ujiyamada, and Tsu.

Note: Underscored cities were bombed with high explosive and incendiary bombs on the night of 28/29 July 1945.

Back of leaflet dropped over Japanese cities and English translation

Front of leaflet dropped to warn Japanese civilians of cities to be bombed

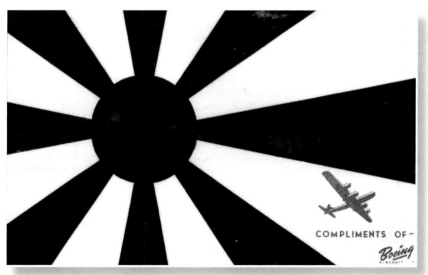

Decals provided for American aircraft that downed Japanese aircraft, compliments of Boeing Aircraft

OSAKA

Osaka aftermath as seen in Brief Magazine

B-29 City of Monroe and Her crew

Daylight formation headed for Japan

Radio operator position in B-29

Prisoner of War supplies dropped by B-29's

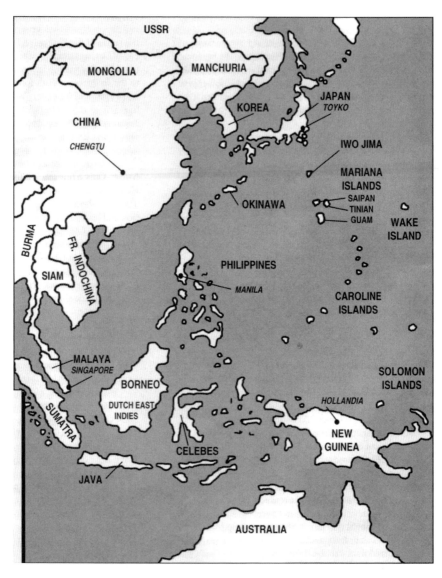

Guam to Japan one-way 1,500 miles

May 29 Yokohama daylight raid-Bombs away

Yokohama daylight raid

May 29 Yokohama night raid results

Bombs dropping during Yokohama daylight raid

More destruction for Yokohama on May 29th night mission

2IBC 5M206 203VI 6-17-1415 12"-8,400 31°32'-130°33' KAGOSHIMA P-25 RESTRICTE

17 June night raid
Kagoshima

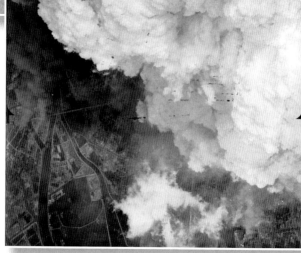

2IBC 5M187 RESTRICTED

7 June night raid
Osaka

Intelligence photo through camera hatch on 5 May target Otake

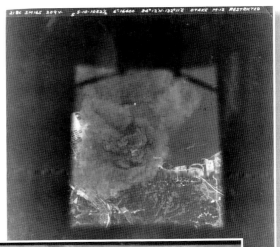

Otake raid with "cabbage head"

7 August raid on Toyokawa

Tokyo display of force 2 September

Silhouette of
Mt. Fuji at sunset

22 June Tamashima Raid

*B-29's
passing
Mt. Fuji in
Japan*

Otake Japan before B-29 raid

*View from
co-pilot's seat of
B-29 formation*

TOKYO was laboratory for the fire-raid technique, got the full treatment several times. Above, a corner of the 56.3 square miles burned.

ONCE the most famous theater in Japan and site of classical plays, the Kabukiza today is a heap of ruins. Photo was taken from stage.

Aftermath of Tokyo from B-29 raids article

Cabbage head of smoke after raid

Pictures of "bombs away" from "Brief" magazine

LIKE LOCUSTS, DOWN THEY SWARM   On 1 June the sky above Osaka was a lovely or unlovely sight to behold, depending on whether you were looking

20

Confidential

Silhouette of B-29 and lights to guide in returning B-29's

*62nd Squadron
39th Bomb Group
B-29 release of
bombs over Japan*

*B-29 with engine
on fire and headed
out to sea*

*Approach of
B-29 to North
Field, Guam*

B-29 ditched in the Pacific

One of the
bomb bays
and tunnel
of a B-29

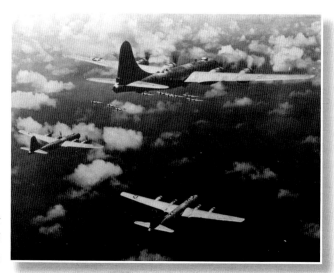

Formation flight
of B-29's headed
for Japan

B-29 in distress with some help from above

B-29 hit and falling over Japan

B-29 "Hells Belle", one of the 39th Bomb Group, 62nd Squadron aircraft

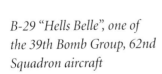

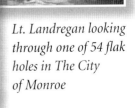

Lt. Landregan looking through one of 54 flak holes in The City of Monroe

Crash landing on Iwo Jima

City of Monroe's 62nd Squadron Formation daylight raid

L to R- Herb and Don Greer at Little Rock Air Force Base, AR

*USS Missouri and
the signing of Japan's
Unconditional Surrender*

Photo of President John F. Kennedy with Don Greer top left, 2nd person

Major Luther Jones (left) meets Herb Greer (right) after 57 years

Registration plate and column cap from B-29 "City of Monroe"

Hart plans to keep his job at DHS

City office opening soon

By MARK CARTER
Leader Staff

The appointment by Gov. Mike Huckabee of Lee Frazier as Department of Human Services head hasn't affected Jacksonville's Roy Hart.

Hart, director of county operations for DHS, said Monday that he was not among the 150 or so DHS employees asked to submit a letter of resignation. He noted that all directors within DHS will eventually meet with Frazier, but that he has "had some indications that (Frazier) is pleased with our division."

Hart said such a transition at the top can be methodical, and while he expects to meet with his new boss to review his division, he doesn't expect to be asked to resign.

"It happens," he said of the change at the top. "I don't think I have anything to worry about."

Hart's division of DHS is overseeing the construction of what will become a new full service DHS office on W. Main in Jacksonville.

He said some interior work remains to be completed, and that an official opening should happen this summer.   (See HART, page 6A)

Herb Greer, a veteran of two conflicts, displays several air medals and other awards and memorabilia, including a model of a B-29, in his Jacksonville home. (Leader photo by David Parker)

Missions over Japan and Korea

Air Force veteran's bombardier in WWII was actor Tim Holt

Herb Greer's collection of memorabilia from the Second World War

By Garrick Feldman Editor

and Korean conflict is spread out on his kitchen table and chairs.

Among scores of items in his Jacksonville home, you'll find a model of a B-29, which he'd flown several times with his brother, Lieut. Donald Greer, who was a co-pilot. A retired lieutenant colonel, his brother now lives at Hilton Head Island, S.C.

The brothers had gone on several missions to Japan, including the firebombing of Tokyo. After the Japanese surrendered, the brothers dropped supplies for American soldiers who were held in prisoner of war camps.

Greer, a former radio operator, has pictures, books, medals, flags and much more to remind him of his 22 years in the Air Force.

"That was the quickest way to get them food, medicine and supplies," Herb Greer says.

During the Korean war, the brothers flew from Japan on 32 bombing raids over North Korea.

Herb Greer's years in the service spanned three wars, ending during the Vietnam era — from B-29s to B-52s to B-47s, the last here at Little Rock Air Force Base.

Greer, 75, who joined the Army Air Corps in 1942, was stationed at Little Rock Air Force Base in 1960 and retired in 1964 as senior master sergeant.

(See FELDMAN, page 7A)

Newspaper article in local newspaper "The Leader" on missions over Japan and Korea

THIS COLUMN CAP & REGISTRATION PLATE
IS FROM A B-29 SUPER FORTRESS
(SERIAL #44-70018) COMBAT ID P-29. THE
PLANE WAS KNOWN AS THE CITY OF 'MONROE' LA'
SHE FLEW TWENTY FIVE COMBAT MISSIONS DURING
WW II IN THE 'AIR OFFENSIVE JAPAN'
SMSgt (RET) HERB GREER SERVED AS
THE RADIO MAN DURING HER MISSIONS

Department of Defense

Korean War Commemoration Committee

CERTIFICATE OF APPRECIATION

is given to

Herbert L. Greer

With deep appreciation for your outstanding service and support
to the United States of America during the Korean War.

"Freedom is not Free"

May 5, 2001

Secretary of Defense

Certificate of Appreciation from Department of Defense, Secretary of Defense, Donald Rumsfeld

Nellie Greer receiving plaque signed by Donald Rumsfield, Secretary of Defense, for her petitioning the Air Force to allow her sons (Herb and Don) to fly on the same B-29 during the Korean War (L-R − Korean Ambassador to the U.S., Herb Greer, Nellie Greer (age 98), Don Greer, Maj. Gen. Nels Running - Executive Director of America's Commemoration of the Korean War 2000-2003

L to R- Herb and son Ron Greer beside B-29 "Fifi"

Herb, 60 years later, in the B-29 cockpit

25 May, 1945

Even though flyers had been dropped, warning them of imminent new raids, the residents of Tokyo would have been forgiven for thinking that the worst was over – what more could the US Air Force throw at them? But on the night of the 25th they were hit by another ferocious raid involving 464 B-29's which dropped a staggering 3,262 tons of incendiary bombs on the financial and commercial districts. Pilots reported that their cockpits were lit up as bright as day due to the fires. The focus was on industry, with rail yards, marshalling areas, factories and warehouses being targeted, but where there was industry there were also the homes of the workers living close by – thousands of them.

The toll exacted from the Japanese people was high, and in turn 26 B-29's were lost. This was the highest loss in a single day during the war. Some of the B-29's lost were Lady Eve, Male Call, Princess Eileen IV (most probably someone's wife, daughter or girlfriend), Hollywood Commando, Shanghai Lil Rides Again, Winged Victory, Peachy, Mammy Yokum and Ramp Queen.

May 26, 1945, Honshu. Target: Tokyo Industrial section eastern part. Hot as hell too, they were waiting for us. We went in to target individually. One Jap twin engine fighter was waiting about 20 miles off the coast and followed us clear in over the target. Flak was very heavy and the searchlights were estimated at about 400 in the Tokyo area; we were in searchlights all the way to the target. Losses were estimated at about 18 B-29's. One crew came back with the tail almost shot off and the tail gunner died instantly. On both raids on the industrial centers, we hit an estimated civilian population of 50,000 to 70,000 people per square mile. Fires were seen 200 miles to sea. Fire looked like it covered a ten square mile area.

We'd hit Tokyo so often, and so hard and for so many weeks that they were definitely expecting us. Tokyo was a vital component of the Nippon machine and we were determined to bring this war to a speedy and proper end. General LeMay had clearly indicated "Burn Tokyo" or you're going back tomorrow.

The searchlights were busy over the target. Later there was a lot of discussion about them with some crews saying that there were as many as seventy-five in the center of Tokyo. Twenty-five more were spotted on the way to the target.

Then we saw him, a twin-engine Jap fighter following us in to Tokyo. He was at the same altitude and air speed. It sure put us on edge as we knew what he was doing. His job was not to try to take us out but to call our position in to the anti-aircraft guns on the ground. We knew, as we got closer, that they would have a bead on us. As we neared the target he veered off and picked up another B-29 entering the target area, once again providing the Jap artillery gunners with the aircraft's altitude and air speed along with prevailing wind conditions.

There were Bakas about too, five of them, although back on my perch I didn't see them myself. Major Jones and DeAngelos saw them though. It was mostly at night when they were around - ready to dive straight at you. We called them Bakas because the word in Japanese means stupid, idiot or fool, and that's what the suicide pilots had to be to fly those things.

The fighter pilot had done his job well because the flak that started to come at us was at first a little above us and then a little below us, but quickly we were in their sights. It was pretty hairy flying through a barrage of exploding shrapnel.

It was a strange feeling when a searchlight picked you out. There you were, cocooned in your dark airplane when all of a sudden it was like somebody turned on all the lights. The feeling of immense exposure is hard to describe, it was like when somebody discovered you doing something naughty as a child, and you just wanted to crawl under a rock and get away from those piercing eyes. Once the searchlight locked on us it stayed on us. There was no way to shake them off – we were center stage, the main act. The ground gunner flak battery would then concentrate on us and the searchlight crew would report our altitude and air speed. Lucky for us the flak, although heavy, turned out to be less accurate than we thought it would be.

Four B-29's were sent in first as pathfinders; they would drop firebombs in a pattern that would indicate a square – the four corners showing us the outer edges of the target area.

We flew in low, one at a time so that we could achieve better bomb concentration and so the coverage would be better – the result was bigger fires. The aim was to hit the outer parts of the square first with later aircraft progressively moving into the center. If any plane missed its target the plane following would hit it, or any area that wasn't already burning. The accuracy was amazing and most times we managed to hit everything within the borders of the target. That was concentration bombing the B-29 way!

As we flew into the target area, maintaining both altitude and airspeed as briefed, the aircraft following us would do likewise some five miles behind and at a thousand feet altitude separation. Flying like this made it more difficult for the ground artillery to hit us. It also prevented us from flying into each other – which on the whole was a good thing!

As if fighters, suicide planes and flak weren't enough to contend with, there were reports of a new red ball parachute flare which threw out tentacles of phosphorus, lighting up B-29's and setting them afire, if they were unlucky enough to be in the path of one.

Hitting the target wasn't easy though. As soon as the target was identified, the bomb bay doors were open and heated air from below rushed up to greet us, making the plane bounce, slip and slide. So, there we were, hoping and praying other aircraft would also maintain their altitude and airspeed as briefed to prevent mid air collision, fighting to keep control, flak flying thick and fast, the smell of burning flesh reaching inside the cabin and a small patch of ground, a few thousand feet below, to try to drop our bombs on. The kids of today play video games where they have to bomb things from the comfort of their sofas, but I wonder how accurate they would be in those circumstances.

As fires built upon fires the heat intensified and the fire became so hot beneath us that it became a firestorm, the fire started to suck in all the oxygen from around it and formed a funnel pulling all the air into itself. This caused powerful thermals to rise and they battered the aircraft like a toy – back at my station I was hanging on for grim life.

As we left the target area and flew out to sea, Tokyo looked like it was enjoying a beautiful sunset – a red glow, forming a half moon. Nothing could have been farther from the truth.

Looking back it's hard to imagine the sheer numbers of people on the ground as the firebombs dropped on them. Hundreds of thousands of people perished that night from the napalm, the fire, the lack of oxygen and the determination of their leaders never to give up, even in the face of such hopeless odds.

I know it sounds strange, but at the time I didn't feel anything – I couldn't let myself feel anything. One of our main targets that night was the Shinagawa Railroad Yards, which were the largest marshalling yards in Japan, but the Japanese had turned homes into mini manufacturing plants and spread them throughout the city so people were making parts for aircraft in their living rooms. Therefore the residential area was also hit. This was war at its most dirty and unforgiving but it was necessary, as a means of breaking the manufacturing chain, in order to bring this conflict to an end.

I also knew what was happening to our boys in the South Pacific and I knew what would happen to us if we were shot down. We had all heard the rumors about what happened to captured fliers; they were tried for war crimes and beheaded on the spot, at the scene of their so-called trial. You and your crew would dig your own grave and the execution would take place at the edge of the ditch so you would just topple in. This made you feel differently about the enemy and it was hard to distinguish between civilians and military targets at several thousand feet.

Our focus was, had to be, to destroy the target as per orders and get out so we could come back and do it again, and again if necessary.

Our Bomb Group got hit pretty hard that night with about a third of our B-29's coming back with heavy flak damage. The crew of the City of Monroe suffered no injuries, but it would have been my job to provide first aid had someone been hit. That was part of the radioman's job so I knew how to wrap wounds and apply a tourniquet. I could also give morphine shots for pain. We did what we could until we reached base and could get the patient into a hospital.

The Baka was actually the Yokosuka MXY-7 Ohka (Cherry Blossom). A flying torpedo shaped aircraft made of wood it had swept-back wings and a small canopy for the pilot. It was almost twenty feet long and had a wingspan of 16 feet. It was difficult to launch and even harder to maneuver for the pilot who was sealed, as though in a coffin, into this flying bomb. His kamikaze mission took place at a top speed of 403 miles per hour and at a maximum dive velocity of 575 miles per hour so he was very difficult to stop. The Baka was carried beneath a medium distance bomber, often a Betty, to within twelve miles of its target and then dropped. Depending on the model, either rockets or a jet engine propelled this flying bomb, with its 2,646-pound warhead, at its target. Often it would fly above B-29 formations and pick out its target and then attempt to ram it. It was a Baka that sank the destroyer Mannet L Abele on April 12, 1945, the first ship to be sunk by this suicide weapon. Fortunately, the mother plane was so slow and ponderous it was very vulnerable to attack by both fighters and bombers. Only 755 of the savage Bakas were ever built and only a relatively small percentage actually took to the air.

There were seven major raids on Tokyo, with the last one on May 25. The city suffered massive loss of life and saw 22.1 square miles razed to the ground on the last two missions alone. By the morning of May 26, the people still alive in Tokyo faced a scene of destruction never before witnessed. More than 50% of the developed part of the city was damaged. Houses, factories, schools – all smashed, burned – whole tracts of land flattened with just a few concrete shells of the larger buildings still standing to remind one that there was once a street, a neighborhood, a store there. And the charred corpses of women and children, still clearly visible, a further testimony. The residents just weren't ready for this; their fire-fighting equipment was antiquated and about as effective against the firebombs as spitting on a forest fire. The B-29 had effectively destroyed everything of importance – Tokyo was released from its bondage only because to continue hitting it would have been a waste of bombs. Tokyo was the largest city in Japan and could be compared size-wise to New York.

The bombers would now move onto other targets and be even more deadly as crews like those of the City of Monroe became ever more experienced in the science of annihilation. The B-29's effectiveness was about to be tested – it took seven raids to bring Tokyo to its knees; how many would it take to destroy Yokohama, Osaka, Kagoshima, Shizuoka, Tamashima, Nobioko, Shimonoseki, Okasaki and the other towns on the Twentieth Air Force's agenda?

29 May, 1945

For Herb and the crew of the City of Monroe, things were just about to get interesting. Their mission was to fire-bomb Yokahama and destroy the main business district which lay along the waterfront. One hundred and one P-51's from the 8th Fighter Command would accompany 454 B-29's on the mission, which would see nine square miles of Yokahama razed to the ground.

May 29, 1945, Honshu. Target: Yokahoma industrial section and warehouses at the docks. Flak was heavy and fires were thick. But we fooled them today. We had P-51 escort and they sure raised hell with the Jap Air Force. They were down shooting the hell out of the Jap planes before they could get off the ground. We saw one Jap Zeke with two P-51's after him. He started rolling after one P-51 had made a pass at him, and a second P-51 rolled after him and gave him a big burst and the Jap never stopped rolling until he hit the ground. We hit the target at 18,500 feet with incendiary. Big fires were started in the Yokahama dock warehouse and industrial area. We got two flak holes while over the target. After we left the target, we escorted ship P-46, Lt Grear, out to sea. He had number 3 shot out over the target and lost number 4 about 150 miles out; we stayed with him, calling the super dumbos when he ditched.

The ship broke into three pieces, all we saw survive were four men. We had to land at Iwo Jima to get fuel and then returned to Guam. 18 hours in the air and was I tired, the ASR (Air Sea Rescue) had arrived when we left P-46. We learned later seven were saved.

This was an interesting mission as it was the first time we had been escorted by fighters. It was really good to see them attacking the Jap planes on the ground before they could even take off! They prowled the docks and the waterfront, strafing the aircraft before they knew what hit them. Any that did get airborne were immediately attacked and brought down. Our boys flew in pairs so that they could protect each other. They would get on a Jap Zeke and hound him until he was down and then go hunting for another.

*It was busy over the target and the flak was all around us. The warehouses
and industrial areas were burning and the P-51's were doing their job. It
looked just like another day at the office when all of a sudden we were hit.
At first it sounded like someone, or something had hit the side; it was far
too loud of a 'thunk' for a bird. We all knew that this was shrapnel, and
that we had been hit by flak. The gunners quickly scanned for damage and
reported back. We had been hit, that was for sure; there were several holes
in the aircraft, but nothing serious had been damaged or so it seemed for
the present.*

*It was then that we saw one of our group in serious trouble. Crippled, with
four Japanese fighters closing in on them, things didn't look good.*

The aircraft the crew saw was P-46; they had run into heavy flak and their
number three engine had been hit hard, seconds later number four engine
was also hit as were the bomb bay doors just as they were closing. The
co-pilot's throttle cables were severed and direct hits on the radio room,
the vertical stabilizer and the fuel transfer system had all but crippled
it. Number three engine was feathered and number four was losing oil.
Their radio operator had been hit by flak entering the aircraft from below.

They headed for open sea but shortly after leaving land, number four
engine was feathered before it could seize up and this, along with the
tremendous drag due to the open bomb bay doors, meant they had to
make plans to ditch. All this with enemy fighters on their tail.

*In the event that an aircraft was in trouble we were briefed that the deputy
lead ship would drop out of formation and protect it, escorting it to safety.
However, as Major Jones looked across he could see that they had trouble
of their own, and were engaged with several Japanese fighters so were in no
position to help anyone else.*

*The P-51's could not protect P-46 due to lack of fuel and had to follow the
navigational B-29 back to Iwo Jima, otherwise they would have had to
ditch in the ocean.*

Lt. Grear (no relation), the Aircraft Commander of the crippled bomber, was calling for help. He needed the protection of our guns. At this point we had to move fast. Major Jones called Holt, our bombardier, and told him to pick a target that wasn't burning and put the bombs on it pronto and let the Japs rot in hell. As soon as we dropped our load we pulled out of formation and positioned ourselves alongside P-46.

We had to lower our flaps, to stay with her because "Slic Chic", P-46, was struggling to maintain the necessary air speed to fly. The Jap fighters had moved to the other side so we assumed a position above and to the right rear where we could protect the ship, and as they maneuvered around the crippled ship so did we. They would seldom attack a fully gunned B-29 with all four engines fully operational. The amazing B-29 could out-maneuver a fighter and with its state of the art gunnery systems, it would have been like taking a knife to a gunfight, as far as the fighters were concerned.

The pilot called us and said he was going to have to ditch. Major Jones urged the pilot to try to make it another 100 miles, but he said he didn't think they would make it with both engines on the right side lost. They were down to between 8,000 to 10,000 feet and struggling to maintain altitude using only the two left engines. To add to the problem their fuel transfer system was damaged to such an extent that they were not able to transfer fuel to the operational engines.

I contacted Iwo Jima and told them that we were escorting an aircraft that was about to ditch and relayed the aircraft's coordinates. In doing this I had to use the code of the day and challenge the receiver and be challenged by them in return. All normal procedures to ensure we were who we claimed to be and they were as well. A short while after, the Slic Chic went down and we circled to protect it until a B-17 'dumbo' showed up with a boat. The boat, containing maps, food and water, a motor and a first aid kit, was dropped. The maps revealed, for navigational purposes, winds as well as currents and were made of silk so that seawater would not destroy them. We circled a few more times and saw four men get into the boat and thought that was all that survived. Later we discovered that three more made it and were picked up by a submarine. Had we not accompanied them and notified Iwo immediately, the crew may have perished.

The crew of the Slic Chic or the 'Old Girl', as P-46 was nicknamed, dumped as many loose items as possible overboard before ditching; they opened all escape hatches and made a beautiful landing with full flaps. However, the plane broke into three pieces on impact and the nose started to go under. The crew, sporting various injuries, made for the life raft, but once on board they realized that there were only seven of them. The B-17 dropped the boat about 60 yards upwind of them, but it took them four hours to reach it through rough seas. There was a note onboard telling them that a submarine was 110 miles away and coming for them. The boat had dry clothes aboard which they immediately changed into.

They could have been forgiven for thinking that their troubles were over. However, the ocean, in the form of a twenty-foot wave, had other plans and sent them all back into the water. Eventually everyone managed to get back into the boat, but it was raining hard and the waves were growing in size. The men were continually thrown overboard all night and in the words of one of them, "we don't expect to get through another hour…the sea is beating us to death and we expect the boat to break up…everyone is praying".

As Herb headed back to base, the next several hours were traumatic for the seven people he had helped. Howard Howes, the navigator, was thrown twenty feet from the boat, but as the next wave brought him back into reach he was grabbed by the hair and dragged back on board. The survivors were indiscriminately thrown from the boat and on one occasion the radar officer, Ralph Hayenga, went overboard and was hauled back by his broken arm. Apparently he never flinched.

It was six hours before they spotted the submarine heading toward them at full speed. Of the eleven man crew only seven survived. They were one of seven B-29's lost on that mission.

After our detour, we were low on fuel and headed for Iwo Jima. It took quite some time before we could get refueled because at that time the underground fueling system wasn't in place. The fuel trucks had plenty of B-29's to service so we had to wait our turn.

It was then that an American Red Cross truck—a sight for sore eyes—- drove over and offered us coffee and donuts. We were tired and after what we had been through on this mission, coffee, and donuts was as good as it gets. Tucking in to this veritable feast, you can imagine my surprise when we were charged for these refreshments. I was totally dumbfounded that after risking our lives to escort a fellow B-29 to safety here we were being charged for "coffee and donuts" by this American institution. I have never forgiven the Red Cross for that day, and to this day have little time for the organization.

The delay in getting back to our base on Guam was of great concern to our ground crew who thought they had lost us. When we eventually arrived home they were very glad to see us!

Back at base they were talking about a super dumbo who was off the coast of Japan looking for survivors. It got a message from a sub that there was unfriendly aircraft close by and that they were going to submerge. The B-29 spotted the Japanese floatplane and shot it down. Our boys circled and went back, the sub then re-surfaced and congratulated them on their sharp shooting! It was always nice to hear of B-29's doing well and we were proud to fly these incredible airplanes. The camaraderie between B-29 crews was quite something!

The crew of the City of Monroe was awarded the Distinguished Flying Cross, a Presidential citation, for this mission and they forever referred to it as their "coffee and donuts" mission.

SECTION V

AWARD OF THE DISTINGUISHED-FLYING CROSS—By direction of the President, under the provisions of the Act of Congress, approved 2 July 1926, and pursuant to authority delegated by Headquarters United States Army Strategic Air Forces in letter, file AG 323, subject: "Definition of Administrative Responsibilities", dated 15 September 1945, announcement is made of the award of the Distinguished-Flying Cross to the following named officers and enlisted men of the 62nd Bombardment Squadron, 39th Bombardment Group.

For extraordinary achievement while participating in aerial flight 29 May 1945. These individuals were members of the combat crew of a B-29 aircraft on a devastating, medium altitude, daylight incendiary strike against Yokohama, Japan. From the initial point until long after the bombs were dropped, their formation was subjected to a shattering concentration of continuously-pointed flak, which scored several hits on their bomber, and to vicious attacks by ten fighters. Despite their fierce opposition however, these crewmen, with outstanding courage and skill, maintained their aircraft exactly on the briefed heading right to the target without resorting to evasive tactics. At the target they dropped their bombs accurately on the briefed aiming point with devastating effect. While the formation was still under intense enemy fire, they left the comparative safety of the formation to escort a severely damaged Superfortress which could not stay in position. Thereafter, until the coast of Japan was left behind, they repeatedly repulsed attempts by enemy planes to bring down the damaged B-29. When the crippled bomber was ditched this crew circled the survivors and called in its position to a Dumbo, until rescue craft appeared on the scene. The courage and fortitude displayed by this veteran combat crew, together with their outstanding professional skill, was instrumental in saving the lives of the survivors of a ditched crew, and reflect the greatest credit upon themselves and the Army Air Forces.

2nd Lt. Howard L. Howes, the navigator of 'Slic Chic' P-46, wrote a letter to the parents of S/Sgt Laurence V. Toeppe, the left gunner, who was one of the four crew members who did not survive the mission.

Letter to parents of Larry Toeppe:

Guam Air Depot
Tues. Feb. 12, 46
Dear Mr. & Mrs. Toeppe:
      Having received your nice letter, I'll have to admit that I am deeply embarrassed that I hadn't written you sooner. I thought surely some of the fellows that have returned to the States would have seen you by now and would have given you the complete terrible story of one most unfortunate

experience. The complete and true story can come only from one of us "lucky ones" that survived. Knowing that you as well as the other boys parents want the true details of all of it, I'll take this time to give them to you as well as I can. This is hard to write and very unpleasant to read. I'll be frank as that is the best way to say what has to be said.

Our experience was terrible, dreadful, horrible and one that we try to think very little about. That part we all hope will he forgotten someday, but the memory of these fine fellows we lost, and how nice all were, will never be forgotten.

Not knowing how much of the story you already know I'll start at the beginning and tell it all. We were on our ninth bombing mission on the 29th of May 1945 against Yokohama, Japan. Over the target we were hit and hit hard, by enemy flak. The plane was pretty well full of holes and two engines on the right wing were knocked out, but luckly only one man was injured due to the flak. Sgt. Schutzman, our radio operator received a piece of flak through his foot. He was very well taken care of and was in high spirits, all through our experience. Because we had two engines out, we were unable to maintain altitude and knew at once we had to ditch.

(Ditching is what we call landing in the water.) The spirit of the crew was always fine, no one seeming scared or loosing his head. We talked and joked until we hit the water.

Under the circumstances, we did a fine job of ditching the plane. Due to the large waves and the roughness of the sea, our plane broke into four parts when we hit. Now each man has his own experience during the ditching, mine of little importance to you, so I'll try and tell you exactly what happened to Larry. He, with three others, was braced in his respective ditching position - Their positions were near the tail end of the plane.

When we hit, a large swell caught the tail of the plane and snapped it off immediately. Those four men really took a terrible shock from which only one survived. The one man saved from the tail of the plane swam a couple hundred yards with one arm as he had a broken collar bone. One man went down immediately, no one seeing him or knowing how badly he was hurt.

Larry and Sgt. Markowitz came out of the wreckage but looked as if they were semi-conscious and pretty badly injured. We remember seeing Larry in the water and apparently trying to hold onto to the wreckage of the plane. As the wreckage of the plane sank, Larry went down with it. No one can say how badly he was injured, but he must have been. Upon hitting the water the front of the plane continued on about one hundred yards. The men in front were as busy as we could be getting the life rafts out and inflated. As soon as we could we all started paddling toward the tail section, which at that time was just sinking. On the way we picked up Lt. Hayenga. When we got to where the tail section was, no one else could be found. We searched until dark all over the place and two planes above us were doing their best trying to find more men still afloat. Yes Larry undoubtedly was injured upon ditching and not being completely conscious was unable to swim or float. Certainly all help that was possible at the time was given him.

Two others drowned that were in the tail section and one from the front of the plane.

I know this is very unpleasant to read but its how it happened and I thought you would like to know the exact details.

The story goes on to say that the ones of us that got into the rafts were just beginning our trouble. With one man with a broken collar bone and one with a flak hole through his foot we were in a bad spot to survive during the night. Waves, and big ones too, kept turning us over all during the night, but by some miracle of God we won the battle and near sundown the next day we were picked up by a submarine.

I intend when I return to the States to visit each family and tell the story more completely and answer each question they have. This is close to being the complete story but I know all will have some questions to be asked. But Mr. & Mrs. Toeppe you asked in your letter if there is any hope. As much as I hate to say it there is none.

Larry as well as all the boys on the crew were fine men. We had a job to do when we came over. Some had to go down dying to complete this job. The job is over now and I know if Larry and the thousands of others were alive today they would be happy to know that there lives had much to do to help bring about this World Peace once again. It's terrible for the families back home and things like this hurt us deeply out here. We didn't go into all this blind folded. We knew the stakes and were ready to give our lives to accomplish what we did. I know Larry felt this way too.

We had the best crew in the Group and it was a great shock to everyone when we didn't return. But the ones of us that returned stayed on helping to finish the jobs we knew the boys that we lost would want us to and since then we personally had more to fight for.

All the other fellows are now back home. I hope to be back by Summer. My job now is flying cargo instead of bombs to Japan. I see Yokohama on every trip and can't help to think of our mission there. We did a fine job that day and you know the city was completely destroyed in one raid. That raid is going down in history on the best single raid in this war.

Under the circumstances I'm sorry that I was on it, but since I was I'll have to admit that I am proud of what we did to Yokohama that day.

It was a pleasure to receive your letter and if there is any further information or help I can give you feel free to write me. I'll also be glad to hear from you. With my deepest regrets for everything.

I remain,

Lt. Howard L. Howes

A FANATICAL FOE
(JUNE 1945)

CHAPTER SEVEN

We have room in this country for but one flag, the Stars and Stripes.

—Theodore Roosevelt.

32,542 tons of bombs dropped

9,954 tons High Explosive; 22,588 tons Incendiary

5,581 sorties, 5,243 effective[5]

June 7 1945 (HONSHU)
Mission #8 OSAKA target osaka
arsenal approximately # 50 B29a
participated in this raid we
took of 5 A.M. morning of seventh
and arrived at our assembly point
ahead of time but thinking we
were late we went on in and
to our amazement found we were
early we started to tack on to

---

[5] http://www.ww2guide.com/b29ops.shtml

NEWS

The June 11, 1945 edition of Time Magazine interviewed Major General Curtis LeMay and he summarized the damage done to Tokyo to date. He said that 51.3 square miles, or 46% of the city had been destroyed, leaving 4.5 million people homeless. In the process, he reported that fifty B-29's had been lost, one for every square mile destroyed.

The United States, Britain, the Soviet Union and France sign the declaration of German defeat in Berlin, Germany at 1800 hours. The signatories are: Dwight D. Eisenhower, General of the Army, USA; Zhukov, Marshal of the Soviet Union; B. L. Montgomery, Field Marshal, Great Britain; De Lattre de Tassisny, Général d'Armée, French Provisional Government.

Japanese forces on Okinawa face a hopeless situation and commit suicide in large numbers. The U.S. Army and U.S. Marines, assisted by the 7th infantry division, capture Okinawa, at a cost of 112,000 Japanese and 12,500 American dead along with 36,000 wounded.

Fifty nations gathered in San Francisco on June 26 to sign the World Security Charter which formally established the United Nations. The name of this new organization originated with President Roosevelt when he identified, four years earlier, the countries fighting against the axis earlier in the war. The United Nations replaced the League of Nations, which was started in WWI under very similar circumstances and ceased to exist after it failed to prevent WWII.

At the movies, back in the States, Danny Kaye is keeping morale high by singing and dancing his way through 'Wonder Man' with Virginia Mayo; and Zachary Scott and Betty Field star in the drama 'The Southerner' which tells of the hardships undergone by a cotton farming family.

The early days of June saw two missions, one on the first and another on the fifth that involved over 900 B-29's attacking Osaka and Kobe, cities the size of Chicago and Baltimore respectively. Herb didn't fly on either day which was probably fortunate as ten B-29's and 27 P-51's were lost on the first day of the month, due primarily to bad weather. The fighters were flying blind and several must have collided with each other; others became lost or were driven to the deck by the terrible weather. Twenty-four fighter pilots were lost on that single day, which made it the largest weather related loss of the war.

One of the B-29's from 869th Bomb Squadron, 497th Bomb Group was hit in the number one engine over the target and was then shot down by fighters south of Osaka. Seven of the crew died in the crash and four were captured. Two were executed immediately, another was killed 19 days later and the last survivor was executed on the last day of the war. B-29 crews could expect no leniency from the Japanese if captured.

Over Osaka on that first day of June, there were plenty of near misses. The cloud cover was thick and the smoke over the target was worse. Flak was being thrown up into the smoke and there were a lot of bombers over the target. One eyewitness tells of another B-29 hurtling straight at them, its tail almost scraping their aircraft.

On 5 June, the B-29's were back in action, dropping 3,077 tons of incendiary bombs on Kobe. Four square miles were burned and damage was reported to encompass more than half the city. Eighty-six Japanese fighters were shot down by B-29's and eleven B-29's were lost.

One aircraft, "Black Jack Too," was hit and had number three engine on fire when two fighters attacked it. They managed to down the first fighter and damage the second, but after limping along for about 15 miles with their wing ablaze, it was seen to buckle and break off. The aircraft rolled onto its back and went into a vertical nose downspin.

Although most of the crew survived the crash they were arrested and taken to Tokai Military Command. Of the ten survivors one was seriously wounded and died the next day. The remaining nine crew members were executed on 28 June, 1945 in the forests of Akatsu-cho, Seto-city.

At least 28 crew members of these downed aircraft are known to have been executed. Others were missing in action or are known to have died in POW camps.

Even those killed in action were given no mercy. The six crew members who died after "Assid Test II" was hit by anti-aircraft fire and crashed, had their bodies burned to ashes and buried in the dry river bed of the Nagi river. It was not until after the war that their ashes were transferred to a public cemetery in Sayama Village, Kuze County.

It was against this backdrop that the young Staff Sergeant Herb Greer was fighting his war. Twenty-three years old, newly married and not much more than a boy, he was facing the horrors of a war like no other. Serving his country by destroying military installations and taking the war into the homes of millions while facing the ultimate penalty if caught. He could have been forgiven for thinking that his future at that point looked bleak. The prospect of being shot down was bad enough, but to survive only to be summarily executed was beyond what other young men normally had to face when going to war. The sacrifice made by these flyers was extraordinary, and in the early days of June it was just beginning. If the young Greer thought it had been tough so far, it was due to get a whole lot worse.

At least one member of every crew of a downed B-29, during those first few days of June, 1945, was executed and in some cases it was the fate of nine out of the eleven crew members.

7 June, 1945

On this day, a staggering 409 B-29's attacked Osaka with 2,592 tons of incendiary bombs. They hit the east central section of the city, targeting industrial and transportation targets. These included the Osaka Army Arsenal, which was the largest munitions storage facility in Japan.

The sky is heavy and the clouds are low so bombing is by radar. Even so, two square miles of the city of Osaka is burned out and over 55,000 buildings are destroyed. Only two B-29's and one P-51 are lost. In the greater scheme of things these losses were far fewer than might have been expected, especially when compared to previous missions this month.

> June 7, 1945 (Honshu) Mission #8. Osaka. Target Osaka arsenal. Approximately 450 B-29's participated in this raid. We took off 5 AM morning of seventh and arrived at our assembly point ahead of time. But thinking we were late we went on in and to our amazement found we were early. We started to tach onto some Saipan planes, but they were headed for a different section or target, so we left them and went in alone....and bombed our target. Bombs away at 11:42 AM. We left the target area without opposition and returned to Guam without mishap. Second home from the raid. Fire bombs.

This was where the City of Monroe really showed her colors. She simply flew faster at the same power setting than the other B-29's and we arrived early, not that we knew that when we arrived over Osaka.

When we arrived we circled several times, but still could not locate our group. We encountered some planes out of Saipan, but they were headed for a different section of the target so we left them to it and decided to hit our target alone. We weren't bothered by any enemy aircraft – they had difficulty keeping up with our B-29's speed.

We went in, dropped our bombs and headed home thinking that we had missed the show. It wasn't until we were back at base that we realized that we had been in and out before any of the others had even arrived over the target. What a sweet plane the City of Monroe was; the power setting, the turbo setting – everything worked so well.

Later, Major Jones was militarily chastised by the other commanders that took part in the raid because he was already home and in bed before the rest of them even got back to base.

9-10 June, 1945

Herb and his crew were having a well-deserved rest for a few days in the second week of June, but the action never stopped. On the 9th, five missions were flown involving 136 B-29's. The Kawanishi Aircraft Company's plant was attacked at Narao. The Kawasaki plant at Akashi is targeted but the village of Akashi is also hit as bombing was by radar. On the same day Aichi's Atsuta factory is hit, but only four bombs are on target; one causes a major fire. Other planes mine the Shimonoseki Strait.

On 10 June, a seaplane base is attacked at Kasumigaura, the Japan Aircraft Company factory at Tomioka is hit and more than 100 B-29's destroy the Hitachi Engineering Works at Kaigan. In total almost 200 B-29's complete six missions.

11 June, 1945

June 11, 1945, mission Rota, load 10 500-pound G.P.s, (general purpose high explosives) bombed airstrip and roadway, direct hit, flight-time 1 hr.

We had experienced some problems with the aircraft, possibly being over weight, so Major Jones had requested her weight to be checked and found she was 1,000 lbs. over her basic weight. We flew her on a mission to Rota to swing the compass in order to set the weight in line with the aircraft navigational and Norden bombsite parameters. This had been requested since the previous mission when Major Jones used all, and then some, of the runway in our take off and took a few palm branches with him as well. We later congratulated Major Jones for his contribution to, and participation in, the "Keep Guam Beautiful Campaign" through pruning the trees.

12 June, 1945

June 12, 1945. Hot rumors still going strong on Jap task force, intercepted by the Navy, attempting to make an invasion on Guam. 12 Jap paratroop transport planes shot down. Everyone is issued extra ammo and we are packing arms at all times. Looks as though there may be some excitement yet.

Japanese paratroop-carrying aircraft were sighted close to Guam, which put everyone in a state of high alert. We were all expecting some action and had been issued extra ammunition. In the end, the Navy aircraft shot them down and prevented any chance of an enemy invasion. We all seem to be getting a little edgy; the long monotonous missions will do that to you.

15 June, 1945

Osaka and Amagasaki were the targets for 444 B-29's carrying 3,157 tons of incendiaries and high explosives. Osaka gets another two square miles razed to the ground and Amagasaki a half-square mile. Twenty-five other aircraft attack other targets. Two B-29's are lost, one crashed only 12 miles north of Guam, almost home, and all eleven crew members were lost at sea.

June 15 1945 (Honshu). Anniversary of first B-29 raid on Japan. Mission #9, target Osaka, Japan; takeoff 2:30 AM for target. Another incendiary raid. 29-each 500-lb incendiary bomb was our load; about 520 B-29's participated in the raid. We made a very good takeoff with our weight being 135,785 lbs. Our flight to Iwo Jima was good, but from Iwo on we ran into trouble. We were briefed that there was a weather front north of Iwo, but not as bad as we found it to be. We were in 10/10 coverage for over 3 hours. We iced up, the tails and wings were covered with ice, and the props were over half coated with the stuff. It finally got so bad that we could only get 165 mph indicated airspeed with max power of 2400 RPM and 43 inches of manifold pressure. We were getting close to the target area and the plane was getting worse. It became very clumsy and sluggish and the pilots had to fight like mad to keep it in level flight. We kept on and finally reached the target alone after floundering around to get there. The weather was still bad as ever, and we made a radar run on the target and dropped our bombs. Then our radar set went haywire. We then retraced our course back through the front to safe air. Boy, I was sure glad to get out of that. For awhile, it looked awful bad for us as the wings and tail were so heavy; I thought sometimes that they would break off the way they bent down. We were running low on gas due to icing making us use more power so we had to land at Iwo Jima where we took aboard 2000 gals. of gas and returned to our home base at Guam. We were told when we got back that P-51 Mustangs were sent to the target for protection, but they never got there due to the horrific weather front.

The weather front was not forecasted to be very bad, but they were wrong – it was real bad. We arrived at the assembly point, northwest of Iwo, before the rest of our group and circled waiting for them to join us. As we had to keep radio silence we could not check in with them to see where they were. After a while Major Jones decided that we had probably missed them and we proceeded on to the initial point where we would start our bomb run. Nothing seemed to go right on this mission; we understood there would be a fighter escort; P-51s were supposed to be following a lead B-29 to Osaka but they never turned up. We never found out what happened for sure but the rumor was that the weather was too bad and several of them ended up crashing into the ocean.

On every mission, we had to deal with one or two weather fronts with thunderheads; it was an everyday occurrence. We never felt comfortable around them though; they could tear an aircraft apart if you weren't careful. We had been briefed that today we would hit a front north of Iwo and we did. It was just a lot stronger than we'd been told. After three hours we were still fighting our way through it and it was getting worse.

Ice was building on the horizontal stabilizer and wings, as well as the propellers, causing tremendous drag. Visibility was down to nil and we were flying by radar. We were feeling pretty lonely up there at that moment. The aircraft was already overweight and now the ice was adding more. I observed the propellers and they looked like huge fence posts rather than the carefully engineered aerodynamic works of wonder they were supposed to be. As for cutting through the air currents they weren't doing a real good job at that moment. The City of Monroe was becoming sluggish and her air speed was sagging markedly. At 165 miles per hour we were some 30-50 miles per hour slower than the aircraft would normally have been travelling, given our throttle settings and the wind speed.

Somehow we managed to get over the target and perform a radar run, dropping our bombs as close to the target as possible under the circumstances. Visibility was still nil so we headed back along the same course we had come. Here we were, one aircraft among over 400 and we had not seen another plane. They were there, they had to be, but we just couldn't see them. It is frightening to be sharing the sky with hundreds of unseen 135,000 lb. masses of metal full of explosives, all heading in the same direction and aiming for the same two square miles of land below. How we never crashed into each other I'll never know!

Once we delivered our payload the aircraft should have gained altitude but it wasn't climbing because of the constant icing and she was becoming unstable. It was all we could do to maintain our air speed. As we started to leave the bad weather, solid ice coated the plane. The weight was incredible and I was getting very concerned. I looked across at Lt. McGuire, the navigator, and he was frozen in position – he just didn't know what to do. We seriously began to wonder whether the aircraft was going to hold together, things were not looking good. As was customary for me, I started praying and my life thus far flashed by me, my mother, my wife, Don my brother and the rest of the family. Eventually we hit warmer air and the ice began to melt. This allowed us to power down as we were burning fuel at a tremendous rate. Then a huge chunk of ice broke free from one of the props and slammed into the side of the fuselage. Now we had a whole new problem; the prop that lost the ice was now unbalanced and the whole engine was vibrating crazily. Major Jones adjusted power on that engine and held the power on the others, juggling the throttles to keep us flying straight as each prop became unbalanced in turn as ice started to melt back into harmless water, but not before it put the fear of God into us.

The entries above illustrate the intense nature of a mission when nature took over from the Japanese as the enemy. Medals are given out for acts of bravery, for saving the lives of fellow airmen, or success in destroying enemy placements. But, in reality, the sheer magnitude of what these crews had to face regularly on days like this deserved a medal. The courage and skill displayed by the crew of the City of Monroe in dropping their bombs on target and bringing a $600,000 (as of 1945) aircraft home safely, in spite of horrendous weather conditions, was amazing.

From the Japanese perspective the raids leading up to this day were ruthless. The local newspaper, the Osaka Asahi, estimated that 70% of the city was destroyed in the four raids prior to 15 June. The chief of air defense in Osaka, Sadaharu Yuasa said that his estimate was only 53%. It is hard using percentages, to appreciate the true extent of human misery this level of destruction brought to the population of Osaka. Whether the newspaper exaggerated or not, it is known that 318,920 houses were burned down in the raid, 10,257 people were killed and 27,224 were wounded.

17 June, 1945

Kagoshima, Omuta, Hamamatsu and Yokkaichi urban areas were hit on 17 June by 452 B-29's. Other B-29's mined the Shimonoseki Strait and the waters around Kobe again. Only one B-29 is lost, its entire crew killed in action.

Mission #10 Target Kagoshima Japan June 17, 1945 (KYUSHU). Mission was very good and great damage was done. We hit Kagoshima about midnight of 17th. Target was visually bombed. Great fires were started and enveloped a large portion of the town. Flack was heavy due to our low altitude attack and there were quite a few searchlights. There was one flack battery of light automatic weapons in the center of town when we went over. It was completely surrounded by fire. Our bomb load was 184 ea 100-pound Gelatin Bombs. The Gelatin when scattered, will stick to anything it strikes and burn there with an intense heat. Smoke over the target was at about 12,000 feet, and we went through it. It was terribly rough due to the thermals in it and bounced us all over the sky. When we released our bombs a couple struck the front bomb bay doors and bent them so that we couldn't get them shut. Tim & I shut them with the emergency system out in the bomb bay. Some fighters followed us out from the mainland but finally left us. Return trip was made without mishap. An incident occurred on the way back though when I turned on my receiver to the emergency frequency. I heard a sub calling a dumbo explaining that someone had crashed in the sea (awarded the Air Medal today).

Herb had quite an experience on this flight, which is only hinted at in his diary entry of that day. Sixty years later he explained to the authors what happened.

As the bombardier released their payload, a bomb hit one of the bomb bay doors and damaged it. This caused a serious problem. As the doors closed they would not latch and were in danger of falling open again. The extra drag on the plane from the open doors would also increase fuel consumption, meaning that they would not be able to make it back to Guam, and possibly not even Iwo Jima.

Herb and Tim had to take their parachutes off and climb into the bomb bay itself and try to get the doors closed. The problem was that there was a whole lot of open space where the bombs had been, giving only a view of a hostile Japan below and very little space for anyone to work in. And there was no way to attach themselves to the aircraft, which was bouncing around complaining that it was no longer perfectly aerodynamic, while our two heroes were trying to reach the back-up system kindly placed there by the manufacturer. In the normal course of things the bomb bay doors shut by themselves using simple air pressure. To change to the motorized emergency system meant getting onto a catwalk which was on the side of the aircraft behind the bomb racks. This was the same walkway that was used to arm the bombs, but in that procedure the doors were shut and the activity was a whole lot safer.

Tim and I were instructed by Major Jones to get the bomb bay doors closed. This involved going into the bomb bay and moving along the catwalk to where there was an electric motor. It was primarily used to lift the bombs into the bomb bay prior to mission departure. This was also the emergency back up for situations like this. We were hanging on for dear life, no parachutes and nothing for us to attach ourselves to. One false move and we would be sucked out, making one hell of an impression on the city below! The cable was there all right, attached to the electric motor, and close to it a separate cable attached to the bomb bay doors. What we had to do was get hold of the bomb bay door cable and attach it to the electric motor. There was very little space and we were being buffeted around like numbered balls at a bingo parlor, but we eventually managed to connect the wires, activate the electric motor and close the doors. Once they were closed, Tim and I felt a whole lot safer and the old girl, the City of Monroe, felt a whole lot more comfortable with herself.

It was hard for Herb sometimes when he picked up a call for help that he couldn't do anything about. On this day it was a submarine calling for a dumbo, but with the City of Monroe low on fuel, it wasn't their job to go on search and rescue missions.

At the debriefing when they got back the crew was informed that they had been awarded the Air Medal.

AWARD OF THE AIR MEDAL (OAK-LEAF CLUSTER) – By direction of the President, under the provisions of Executive Order No. 9158, and pursuant to authority delegated by Headquarters United States Army Strategic Air Forces in classified letter, file 323, subject: "Delineation of Administrative Responsibilities", announcement is made of the award of the Bronze Oak-Leaf Cluster to the Air Medal as indicated:

For meritorious achievement while participating in aerial flights as combat crew members in successful combat missions against the Japanese Empire. All missions were flown under rapidly changing and, at times, adverse weather opposition. There were constantly present difficult navigational problems, danger of engine failure and consequent ditching many miles out at sea. Under prolonged periods of physical and mental strain, and undaunted by the many hazards faced regularly and continuously, each crew member displayed such courage and skill in the performance of his duty as to reflect great credit on himself and the Army Air Forces.

19 June, 1945

Four missions were flown on this night, involving 508 B-29's. They hit Toyohashi, Fukuoka and Shizuoka with incendiary bombing raids and the total area destroyed was 5.32 square miles. Twenty-eight B-29's mined the Shimonoseki Strait. Three B-29's were lost.

During these missions, two B-29's collided and crashed near the Abe River, about 150 miles south of Tokyo. Two surviving crewmen were found by a Japanese man called Mr. Ito. He tried to help them, but they died of their injuries. Military law decreed that, dead or alive, all enemies were to be turned over to the authorities, but Mr. Ito took it upon himself to give them a Shinto burial, at the base of Mt. Sengen where there was a Shinto shrine. He was later labeled a traitor for these actions and lived in disgrace for the rest of the war. Following the war, he built a monument to the Japanese citizens killed in the raid that night and also attempted to get the names of the Allied airmen so that he could erect a monument to them as well. His courage and spirit of understanding did a lot to create a warm and strong relationship between the Japanese and the Americans after the war.

Mission #11, Target Shizuoka, southeast of Yokohama. Load 40 each 500- pound incendiary bombs; hit the target about midnight of June 19, 1945. Fires were scattered and smoke reached to 15,000 feet. We hit a thermal over the target and gained 2,000 feet instantly. I was in the rear un-pressurized section by the camera hatch waiting to throw out window when we hit it. The next thing

I knew I was plastered against the top of the plane and then down on the floor again with boxes, Gibson Girl (hand-cranked signal box) and everything else bouncing off my head. I lost consciousness for about three minutes. Landregren was hit in the head by a water jug and was knocked silly. He finally came around, and I gave him three aspirin tablets and cleaned a place in the back and made him lie down. I took a big compress bandage and soaked it with water from one of the canteens and kept it on his head. He finally went to sleep. He awoke later, still groggy but feeling much better. Mission was complete without mishap. One B-29 is still missing.

This was a night mission. After we attended our specialized briefings the trucks picked us up. It was time to say goodbye to our friends who weren't flying tonight – as we made our way to the flight line, we waved to them and they waved back, neither knowing whether we would ever see each other again. All of us putting on a brave face.

Once the whole crew arrived at the aircraft we gave the ground crew our personal effects. It was a strange feeling handing over billfolds, identification and whatever else that needed safekeeping, never knowing whether we would be back to collect them again. We did keep our dog tags though. The ground crew were wonderful, not only did they keep our aircraft in tiptop condition but they could always be trusted to look after your belongings. I have to say I would trust them over a bank any day – what great service!

Once I was aboard the plane I started on my ritual of checking everything. No time to worry about the mission, about whether I would ever see my wife again, whether I would ever have children – I switched to business mode. I checked the antennas, radio transmitter and receiver and radio compass to ensure they were working and accurate. I made sure the Gibson Girl, our emergency, hand crank radio was aboard and complete. I checked that we had the correct flares and that we had the required number of them. My pistol was next and I made sure I had ammunition and extra clips. We were often reminded to save a bullet for ourselves in case we were captured. It was either that or execution or vivisection. Or worse.

The missions were long and exhausting. During take off, over the target or in bad weather we were all alert; fear will do that to you. But, when you have spent 12 to 18 hours in the air, mostly over water, the constant drone of the engines tends to lull you to sleep if you aren't careful. Even the anxiety and constant 'what if' thinking couldn't always keep you awake. The question on all our minds was "will this be our last mission?". We could all predict that some of the planes wouldn't come back, but we had no way of knowing which ones. I can honestly say that I did more self-searching, and what I guess would currently be called existential thinking, during those days above the Pacific than anytime before or since.

The Gibson Girl, or the T-74/CRT3 as it was officially called, was an emergency transmitter that Herb would have used to send out an automatic SOS if the City of Monroe had crashed. He would have used a small canister of helium gas to float a balloon to which he would have attached antenna wire before cranking the handle to generate the power to run the transmitter. The Gibson Girl was basically a square box with pinched insides and this is what gave it its nickname, after the slim waisted pin-ups in Charles Dana Gibson's Life magazine.

Once I had checked everything on the inside of the plane, my ritual continued. My next check was the small fuel valve on the bottom of the right wing. This was vital to the success of the mission and probably the most important thing I would do, for two reasons. First, to check for any water in the fuel tanks, but equally important was to fill my Zippo lighter with 140-octane fuel since I would be smoking my brains out during another 16-18 hour mission! As a radio operator I couldn't be relieved so it was extremely important to have a fully operational lighter, an ample supply of cigarettes and a large quantity of coffee.

Once aboard we waited for our engine start time, and then taxied from the hardstand to join a procession of huge silver beasts, nose to tail like elephants in a circus parade. Depending on where we were in the line-up we could look fore and aft and see giant fins stretching into the distance, piercing the failing light.

It must have been an awe-inspiring sight for the crew of the City of Monroe as they slowly moved closer to the front of the line, watching aircraft taking off every 30 seconds on parallel runways. Imagine an airplane, a 70 ton silver beast slowly beginning to move – lumbering down the runway, gathering speed as it gets closer and closer to the point of no return, closer and closer to the edge of the cliff, until every part of its being is straining, fighting gravity tooth and nail until, at the very end of the 8,500 foot runway, fate decides that today it will win its battle with gravity and become airborne.

It was a whole lot different flying combat missions than training missions; sure, we carried bombs when training but never 40 each 500 pounders, along with over 6000 gallons of 140-octane fuel, and 1200 rounds of ammo for each of the 12 .50 caliber machine guns. That was some serious explosives we were sitting on as we headed, engines screaming and every rivet of the plane straining, far too slowly toward the edge of a cliff.

Once we were up in the air we became a completely different animal, no longer a lumbering giant fighting gravity. Now the City of Monroe was in her element, a supremely powerful aircraft, not to be messed with. Talk about road rage today, if anyone got on the wrong side of us, they were going to see some unmistakable air rage.

Today, as it thunders down the runway, we take for granted that the aircraft we are on will take off, but in 1945 the B-29's leaving Guam regularly carried loads that exceeded the manufacturer's specifications by enormous amounts. Getting airborne was never a foregone conclusion for Herb or the crew, especially as they had seen first-hand the results of many disastrous attempts.

On this day the journey to Japan was uneventful, which is more than could be said for the rest of the mission. Herb was part of an event that would see 123 B-29's each drop 20,000 pounds of thermite sticks on Shizuoka, but he and the crew of the City of Monroe had no idea what that meant in terms of sheer destruction.

There were a large number of searchlight beams piercing the sky and flak was bursting all around us. Once the searchlights picked us out they would lock on and follow us through the target and this allowed the anti-aircraft guns below to see us clearly. This was not a good thing, so I was not surprised when I heard the voice of Tim, our bombardier, in my headset telling me he wanted me to throw the window out. This involved entering the tunnel which meant removing my flak helmet and parachute.

When Herb refers to the 'window' he is talking about a box that contained strips of tin foil of various lengths. His job was to throw the strips out of the camera hatch so that they hit the air stream and spread out like a cloud. This was something new to the crew and it was still pretty basic; later aircraft had automatic dispensers that ejected the foil at the flick of a switch. The foil strips had the effect of pulling the searchlights off the aircraft and provided a false target for the anti-aircraft guns. So, that was why Herb wasn't wearing a parachute, or seat belt, when they hit the thermal.

What Herb didn't realize, but was soon to discover, was that the incendiary bombs being dropped were close enough together to create a firestorm. In a firestorm the air above the bombed area becomes exceptionally hot and rises rapidly. At the same time cold air from outside of the fire rushes in at ground level. Temperature above the fire can be between 800° - 3000°. As they flew above the target, ready to drop their bombs, a thunderous rush of air with the power of a tornado soared upward to greet them. It took the City of Monroe and pushed it up 2000 feet, tumbling the aircraft like a toy and with such force that it pinned Herb to the floor of the plane before proceeding to give him the wildest ride of his life.

The funnel that the firestorm formed was like the smoke coming from a chimney. When we hit it, it caused our plane to gain 2,000 feet in altitude in a matter of seconds. Everything that wasn't secured was flying all over the place, much of it bouncing off my head.

I thought at first that we had been hit by anti-aircraft fire or possibly been

*rammed by a fighter or Baka. It was some time later that we discovered
that we had been hit by a whole lot of hot air!*

Herb was thrown around like a rag doll and knocked unconscious
for about three minutes. When he came round he discovered that
Landregan, the radar officer, was unconscious and bleeding. Herb
rendered first aid and put a large compress bandage on Landregan's
head and soaked it with water. It wasn't until after he had dragged him
to safety, beyond the pressurized door, that Herb realized he too was
bleeding from a head wound.

Robert Landregan was a 2nd Lt & Radar Officer from Chicago, Illinois
where his father worked with the Railroad. He was in his early 20's when
flying aboard the City of Monroe, and was an Engineering graduate from
Purdue University in Indiana.

Other B-29's experienced similar phenomena. One airman told how
they were turned completely upside down in a thermal and had to
undertake a downward half-loop in order to pull the aircraft out of the
"twister-like" centrifugal force created by the firestorms. The pilot and
co-pilot had to put their feet on the instrument panel and use every
ounce of strength they had to pull the control yoke back. The B-29, as
advanced as it was, didn't have power assist so muscle power was all they
had to rely on – it was either that or a fiery grave. They were close to the
ground before they managed to get the plane right side up.

It was at times like this that crews had to rely on instinct to survive. No
amount of training could prepare you for something like that and it
happens in an instant. For that crew caught in a thermal with the power
of a Kansas twister the choices were limited; turning the plane was not an
option as it would have gone into a spin, they couldn't bail out because
they were upside down in the center of a twister and they couldn't even
ditch the aircraft and jump, because the escape hatches were in the wrong
position. In the end, on this occasion, they made the right decisions and
luck, good fortune or fate was on the side of the good guys.

That aircraft was destined to never fly again though, because the strain
on the wings had been so great they had actually bent. After it landed at
Iwo, the plane was in such a bad state that it had to be scrapped for parts.

We had plenty to talk about the next morning at the debriefing. Two officers wanted chapter and verse on the mission. They wanted to know how many fighters we had seen, how many searchlights and batteries, did we see any damaged aircraft and also how effective was the 'window'. Well, I'm not sure how much help I was as my poor old head had taken a beating and I'd spent part of the time over the target bouncing off the sides of the aircraft and having my head used like a cue ball in a game of billiards.

22 June, 1945

Three hundred and eighty one B-29's took part in six missions on this day and hit the Kure Naval Arsenal damaging 72% of its roof area; the Mitsubishi plant at Tamashima, destroying half the machinery and buildings; the Kawanishi aircraft plant at Himeji, destroying most of its buildings and all the machinery; the Mitsubishi and Kawasaki aircraft plants at Kagamigahara and the Kawasaki aircraft factory at Akashi.

Five B-29's are lost. One crashed soon after take-off while trying to return to Guam with engine problems and only one crew member survived. Maximum Effort III was shot down just offshore of Gobo City after it had bombed the Mitsubishi aircraft factory – all the crew were killed in action. Another plane was attacked by Japanese fighters and crashed in Nagashima Town; two of the crew died in the crash and nine were taken prisoner. All nine were beheaded at Tokai army headquarters three weeks later. A fourth B-29 was shot down by anti-aircraft fire and crashed in Yoshino, Kanda-cho, Kochi City. Seven members of the crew were killed in action and four were captured, one of who died later that night of his wounds. The remaining three were moved to Kure naval headquarters and then onto Ofuna POW camp where they remained for the rest of the war. The last B-29 faired better than the rest on this day in June. Although they crash-landed on Guam, all crewmembers survived.

So, on one night 44 brave airmen failed to return to Guam and eleven had an abrupt return, but lived to tell the tale.

Mission #12, Honshu, June 22, 1945. Target: Tamashima. A Mitsubishi aircraft factory. We hit the target a little after midday of 22nd, bombs away 12:10. We see quite a few fighters on this raid. One twin engine attacked us, but we drove him off with the 50-calibers. He left us alone after that. On entering target we seen one B-29 shot down by Japs. About six fighters had caught him alone. One other ship was hit and blew up. The target was 85% destroyed. We returned to base without mishap. When we hit the target it was clear, very high clouds. We hit them at about 15,500 feet and dropped 24 each 500-pound GP (general-purpose) composition B demolition bombs. Hits were very good, you could see smoke from the target at about 10,000. We saw the smoke above the target over 75 miles away. All in our group returned safely.

We saw a plane hit and explode, we looked for parachutes, but knew that if you're hit bad, your bombs and fuel explode and you have no chance to bail out. In this case the ship was spinning out of control and the centrifugal force would be pinning the crew against the airframe, preventing them from escaping. Not a nice way to go.

Herb refers to composition B demolition bombs. These contained 60% RDX (Royal Demolition Explosive) which is a chemical called Cyclonite, 39% TNT and 1% wax.

The mission went off without too much trouble and we didn't lose anyone in our group. The weather was clear, the flak not too bad and we got in and out quickly.

This mission was pretty standard and it is curious to note that although Herb's plane was attacked by a fighter and he saw another B-29 shot down, this is all taken as just part of another day. The crews were by this time quite hardened to the facts of combat life.

On the way home I picked up Tokyo Rose. When you are stuck in a tin can

for 18 hours at a stretch staring at the radio your boyish curiosity takes over. We all knew that she was broadcasting propaganda but we didn't care, we enjoyed the current popular songs and music she played. For me she made the long trip home a little more bearable.

The name Tokyo Rose was a GI invention and was often applied to several different female voices broadcasting on Japanese radio during the war. An American woman, Iva Ikuko Touri, born in Los Angeles of immigrant Japanese parents, was forced to broadcast propaganda during World War II, despite continually trying to return home to the United States. It was she who became known as Tokyo Rose.

Her show was called The Zero Hour and she played current favorites like 'Speak to me of Love' and 'Loves Old Sweet Song'. They were meant to make the GI's homesick and with comments such as "Are you enjoying yourselves while your wives and sweethearts are running around with the 4F's in the States?" The show almost certainly had an effect on some of its listeners.

There are many stories about her and some are undoubtedly more legend than fact but the bottom line is that she became only the seventh person in the history of the United States to be found guilty of treason. She was sentenced to ten years in prison and fined $100,000. She only served six years and two months of her sentence and successfully fought government efforts to deport her. She applied for a presidential pardon both in 1954 and 1968 before finally being granted one on January 19, 1977 by President Gerald Ford.

At about this time the crew of the City of Monroe were making news back home in Louisiana. The Times-Picayune talked about the 27-year old Louisianian, Major Luther A. Jones commanding the City of Monroe. The crew were called hard-hitting as they "chalked up a mighty record over Japan". Tim Holt got a mention as a film star and an outstanding bombardier, having dropped 143,900 pounds of bombs on Japan in a matter of only five weeks.

The newspaper reported that the crew was in high spirits and that they were predicting the war would be over before the end of 1945, based on how much of Japan had been bombed and burned off the map. They quoted Major Jones as saying "when these 500 and 1,000 B-29's start attacking the three islands of Japan proper every day, day after day, there's not going to be much left of Japan. They are just getting a taste of what the future has in store for them."

The reporter commented on Major Jones' flaming red baseball cap which had 12 miniature bombs painted on the peak.

The newspaper went on to report that he had been overseas for just over two months, but had already flown 36,000 miles and been in the air for 192 hours.

26 June, 1945

There were nine missions on this day in 1945 involving 510 B-29's and 148 P-51's. They hit aircraft factories, industrial targets and arsenals in Osaka, Akashi, Nagoya, Kagamigahara and Eitoku. Six B-29's were listed as lost. Of these six, only four were accounted for. One was shot down by an enemy fighter at Miyama Village, after bombing the Utsube Oil Refinery. Two of the crew were killed in action and the rest were executed. A second bomber was rammed by a 24-year-old Japanese Army fighter, flown by second lieutenant Yutaka Nakagawa. Accounts differ, but it appears that nine or ten were killed and one or two parachuted and were captured. At least one surviving crew member, the tail gunner, was executed. The two remaining ships were both downed with eight crew members killed and fifteen rescued.

Planes going down and crews being killed was a fact of life for the aircrews in Guam, but what no one could get used to were the tales of American airmen being beheaded, often to allow Japanese soldiers to practice their swordsmanship.

Herb and his fellow flyers had a great deal of trouble understanding the Japanese attitude toward life. Their obsession with executing prisoners of war was seen as nothing short of barbaric and made them seem less than human. The average American put a high value on life and considered every life worth saving. In battle, allied troops would always go back for their wounded whatever the risk. In contrast the Japanese would often kill their wounded, as it was deemed dishonorable to be captured, considering their death a sacrifice for the greater good.

The Japanese lack of value for life was further demonstrated by the fact that suicide was preferable to surrender. The fact that westerners would surrender rather than take their own life made it easy for the Japanese to detest Allied prisoners.

This philosophy of honor dates back hundreds of years and is clearly seen in the Bushido, or 'Way of the Warrior', code of life for the Samurai, the warrior aristocracy of Japan. The code puts emphasis on loyalty, self sacrifice, justice, a heightened sense of shame, refined manners, purity, modesty, frugality, martial spirit, honor and affection"[6]. In fact this code was not dissimilar to that of the medieval knights of England.

To the Japanese, beheading was not the horrific act it was seen as by westerners; it was in harmony with the sentimental and moral values of Bushido.

The Japanese believed that they were of a higher order than westerners and that they lived in the land of God. The sun rose first over Japan and then traveled across the world; thus, the land of the rising sun.

Whatever their justification, Japanese military personnel were in a league by themselves when it came to brutality. You were 17 times more likely to die as a prisoner than in battle against them. They shot their prisoners, beheaded them, hung them by their thumbs over bamboo stakes, drank their blood, ate their livers, beat them and worse. Some prisoners were taken to medical camps and operated on while still conscious, so that student doctors could study their organs while they were still pumping. Others were tied to stakes and shot multiple times, or had shells explode close to them so that the effectiveness of various munitions could be assessed. Surgeons would then practice on these live, but critically injured, prisoners.

The pure scale of the Japanese killing machine was incredible. Japanese troops killed six million Chinese between 1932-1945 in what is often referred to as the hidden holocaust. While laying waste to China they

[6] Nippon the Land and Its People: 1998 (Nippon Steel Human Resources Development Co. Ltd.)

hung up children and let their dogs feed on them while they were still alive, and systematically raped tens of thousands of women.

In the European Theater, approximately four percent of allied troops captured, died while prisoners of war. In Japan, the figure was a staggering 36%.

This was why many aircrews kept a spare bullet in their .45 automatics in case they were captured. The Japanese may have preferred suicide, for them an honorable death, to captivity, but American flyers would often choose it also, rather than suffer the degradations and inhuman treatment handed out by their captors.

28 June, 1945

June 28, 1945 General MacArthur's Headquarters announced the end of Japanese resistance in the Philippines.

During the night of 28-29 June, four missions were flown involving 487 B-29's. Only two were lost. The first two missions attacked Okayama and Sasebo, destroying 63% and 48% respectively. The two bombers which were lost, both crashed in enemy territory with no survivors. The second two missions destroyed 27% of the city of Moji and 36% of urban Nobeoka.

June 28, 1945, mission #13, target: Nobeoko. Take-off 7:00 PM. Hit the target about 3:00 AM in the morning. Bomb load 189 one hundred-pound incendiary bombs. Went over target at 10,000 feet with meager flack and fighter opposition. Searchlights were not used. Maybe none available. Some automatic weapons fire which was harmless and very little heavy flack was sighted, although we got one small flack hole in our bomb doors. Fires were started good when we went over, and spread good. We saw our bombs explode on a dark patch next to one of the big fires. Return from target was good. No fighter or air-to-air bombing.

This was another night mission. It was raining cats and dogs as we checked the aircraft, I remember thinking that if it really were raining cats and dogs

the locals would eat very well tonight. It seemed almost every mission was dogged by severe weather, but at least we became experts at flying through it. We were briefed that our target was a city called Nobeoko which lay on the west side of Kyushu peninsula south of the main island. Our load that evening was 189, 100-pound napalm bombs. More death and destruction.

As was normal for a night mission we weren't going to be flying in formation. Poor visibility and bad weather increased the risk of us colliding with each other, so we were assigned a specific altitude and air speed. We flew in a bomber stream, ten minutes apart with a 1000 feet altitude separation.

As I performed my Zippo ritual, I noticed Tim, our bombardier, with the gunners arming the twelve .50 caliber machine guns. The Browning .50 M2 was a great gun, very reliable with a high muzzle velocity and good ballistic characteristics; we carried twelve in remote controlled turrets. The B-29 had previously carried an additional 20mm cannon in the tail but it had proved too unreliable. Our twelve beautiful Brownings were the reason Jap fighters were never to keen to take on a fully functioning B-29.

The Browning M2 was followed by the M3 and both are still in service today. The Japanese copied the Browning and called it the HO-103, which was lighter and faster but fired smaller rounds.

By the time we had checked everything and hauled ourselves aboard we were all soaking wet. The forecast for the target was not good; we were briefed to expect 8/10 to 10/10 coverage. Another fun day to be flying! Once we reached the Initial Point and headed for the target the weather became far worse and we ended up having to bomb by radar.

Resistance from the ground wasn't too bad, some flak and only a few fighters to cause problems, and even though the weather was pretty bad we were able to see our bombs explode through breaks in the cover.

I didn't notice the flak hole until after we landed when we were carrying out our normal walk-around to check for damage. In itself it was small and nothing to worry about, except that it had obviously occurred after we had dropped our bombs and not before. The skin of a 100-pound bomb isn't all that thick and had the flak hit us prior to bombs away it would have almost certainly set them off, sending us into oblivion. That's luck I suppose, it's all in the timing. And, it just wasn't our time.

ENDURING THE UNENDURABLE
(JULY 1945)

CHAPTER EIGHT

The cause of freedom is the cause of God. – W.L. Bowles

42,551 tons of bombs dropped

9,388 tons High Explosive; 33,163 tons Incendiary

6,464 sorties, 6,168 effective[7]

NEWS

Major General Curtis E. LeMay was quoted in the July 2, 1945 edition of Time Magazine as saying "We have destroyed the five largest cities in Japan and any one of these would be a major disaster. We have done this with less than half the strength we will have in the Pacific. We have the capacity to devastate Japan and we will do so if she does not surrender. Missions of 1,000 planes will come before long. ... in a few months we will be running out of targets."

This was the month that the first atomic device was to be detonated. It would take place in Alamogordo, New Mexico, where only a few months previously Herb had been stationed.

The U.S. would deliver its final ultimatum to Japan to cease hostilities or be annihilated. On July 29, Japan would make the mistake of rejecting this offer.

At home, President Truman would receive approbation from the people by way of an 87% approval rating in a Gallup poll for his handling of the war. It is likely this influenced the tough decisions concerning the atomic bomb that he was to make in a matter of weeks. President Roosevelt's highest rating during the war was 84% with a survey post Pearl Harbor.

'Rhapsody in Blue' was wowing audiences back home starring Robert Alda, Oscar Levant and Joan Leslie; while James Cagney in the war thriller 'Blood on the Sun,' played a war reporter in Tokyo who gets hold of secret war plans.

1 July, 1945

The beginning of July saw four bombing raids and one mining raid. More than 550 B-29's took to the air and attacked targets in the urban areas of Kure (40% destroyed), Kumamoto (20% destroyed), Ube (23% destroyed) and Shimonoseki (36% destroyed). Herb's 314th Bomb Wing attacked Shimonoseki, losing one aircraft with five more being hit. Details are sketchy on many of the downed planes but we know that the crew of an aircraft from 19th Bomb Group abandoned their plane northwest of Iwo Jima with their engines on fire. Two men were missing in action and nine were rescued.

July 1, 1945, mission #14, target: Shimonoseki. Take-off 7:30 PM, hit the target about 3:30 AM. Bomb load 40 each 500-pound incendiary clusters. Flack was not effective, lots of automatic weapons fire, but it was pooped out and bursting below us. Heavy flack was meager and not accurate. I did not see any Jap fighters and fireballs. When we went over the target, there were large fires burning there, and we could also see fires from the other targets that were hit by other wings. Mission was successful. We returned without mishap. Mission going and return 3,000 miles plus. We landed with 500 gallons of gasoline.

We made our way to the mess hall at around 3:00pm for a late lunch. The food was pretty basic as it would be no good having a spicy or exotic meal that could turn on you at 10,000 feet over the target. It was bombs we planned to drop, not our pants! It sometimes made it hard to chew, knowing that it could be your last meal.

The next job we had to do was attend the briefing session where we were informed that our target was Shimonoseki. We also learned that our bomb load was to be 40 each 500-pound incendiary clusters dropped from 11,000 feet.

The briefing was important as it allowed me to calculate just how many cigarettes I would need for the mission. I had become pretty much an expert by then and could tell within a margin of error of 5 cigarettes how many I would need. This was definitely a two-pack or 40 cigarette mission!

We were scheduled for take off at 7:30pm. As usual we were transported to the aircraft which sat on her hardstand. We carried out a thorough preflight and each of us affectionately patted our lady, knowing that she would be true to us.

Once aboard we sat and waited for our engine start and taxi time. It was all business now, we were on the clock, our business day about to start. Our job was to destroy Japan's ability to wage war – and slowly but surely we, and thousands like us, would achieve our goal.

As we taxied to our take off position, I double-checked my equipment, including my safety belt. In this case there was little need for the military to ensure compliance with a safety belt law, we all knew the penalty for non-compliance and it involved bandages around the head. If an engine was going to fail it was quite likely to do so during the strain of takeoff so safety was a priority right from the start of a mission. Of course, if an engine failed as we headed for the edge of the cliff we would be in the hands of an authority a whole lot higher than the military!

On this day take off was normal, or at least as normal as it could be for Guam, and we climbed to our cruising altitude of 10,000 feet.

Once in the air, it was pretty much routine stuff, not particularly exciting but critical for safe, optimum performance of the aircraft and the success of the mission. Two hundred miles from the Japanese mainland the weather started to worsen and we started another of our rituals – putting on flak vests and helmets. Then it was the regular build-up of anticipation. What would be waiting for us? Would this be the time that flak took an engine out, or a fighter surprised us or a Baka rammed us? At these times an army cot and a Quonset hut sure looked more appealing than a landing in enemy territory for a date with a long sword. Once over target, the weather broke a little which allowed us a view of our bombs hitting their target.

Back at Guam we learned that 36% of the city was destroyed. We and our fellow flyers had done our job. To put this into perspective, Shimonoseki was a city the size of San Diego.

It was significant that the City of Monroe landed, after flying 3,000 plus miles, with 500 gallons of fuel left in her tanks. This would equate to a little over 8% of their total fuel load of 6,000 gallons. A small margin of error when flying thousands of miles over enemy territory and the open Pacific ocean, but truly amazing when considering that the suggested mileage by the manufacturer was as little as 1,600 miles radius for a B-29 loaded with 5,000 pounds of bombs at high altitude and 20,000 pounds at low altitude. During training missions many planes would land on fumes and actually completely run out of fuel as they attempted to taxi to their hardstand.

The reason that Herb's aircraft managed such amazing fuel economy was due to the superior flying skills of Major Jones and Marshall

Goldston, the flight engineer, who stretched mileage to its maximum; never slamming the engines, Jones eased them through each mission and babied them on take-off and in the air.

Men who fly are a clubby bunch. They like to join social organizations, especially of there own creation - and the screwier the better. There is the famous "Caterpillar Club," for instance; all you have to do to acquire membership is to have your life saved by a parachute. In New Guinea, "The Pedestrian Club of Papua" was formed, because so many airmen crashed in those jungle hills that the bush was always full of aviators, walking back to base.

Goldston was a member of the most notable club, the Society of the Short Snorter, a world-wide "club" whose membership rolls contain the names of some of our tortured globe's highest ranking personages - Presidents, Premiers, Kings, etc. As you might have suspected, the "Short-Snorter's" Society started at the nearest bar. Airmen - pilots, navigators, and such - often met others of the sky clan in far off places around the world. Quite naturally, the fraternal spirit of the men who ride the airplanes of the world prompted a quick adjournment to the nearest brass-rail or cafe for (you guessed it!) a short snort.

To become a member in good standing of the Short-Snorters you can't be just any old plane traveler. No, you must prove that you have flown an ocean. The rules of the esteemed organization calls for "a non-stop flight of a thousand miles or more over water." Proof of this qualifying flight must be attested to by at least two members in good standing of the Society. To each of these members the enrollee turns over one dollar and a third is duly inscribed with information such as date, signature of crew members, signature of high ranking personages and other pertinent data. This bill is then kept as a membership card.

The club rules were strict, as Herb tells us.

If you ever forgot your "membership certificate, or accidentally spent it, you could be in real trouble. If you were caught without your certificate bill by another short-snorter, it meant you had to buy a round of drinks for the house.

Marshall Goldston's silver certificate bill featured the 11 signatures of the B-29 crew P-59 "The City of Monroe" on the front and on the reverse side the signatures of Gen. Curtis E. LeMay, Commander of 21st Bomber Command; Gen. Carl Spaatz and Samuel W. Smith believed to be on crew P-57.

2, July 1945

Thirty-nine B-29's from the 315th bomb wing bombed the Maruzen Oil Refinery at Minishima during a night mission.

July 3, 1945 through July 11, 1945. Changing all four engines on our ship, putting on all new ones. Old engines had over 300 hours. No abortions, no scratches, set a record for the 62nd Squadron

3 – 11 July, 1945

Over 500 B-29's, on five missions, took off from Guam on 3 July and destroyed huge tracts of urban areas in Takamatsu (78%), Kochi (48%), Himeji (63.3%) and Tokushima (74%). Twenty-six of these aircraft mined the Shimonoseki Strait and the waters around Funakawa and Maizuru. Four B-29s were lost.

Herb and the crew were out of commission during this period as the City of Monroe's four engines were being removed and sent back to the Dodge Motor Company so that they could be tested. The issue at hand was why they had lasted so long, and been so reliable. The plane had set a record of over 300 hours without a single abort or scratch due to engine problems. This record was not just a squadron record but one for the entire 39th Bomb Group.

Although Herb was out of action, it didn't mean things were any quieter for the people of Japan. In the few days the City of Monroe was out of service, thousands of bombers dropped hundreds of thousands of pounds of incendiary and high-explosive bombs. Urban areas were being razed to the ground at an astonishing rate.

On 6 July, 570 B-29's attack urban areas destroying 43.4% of Chiba, 57% of Akashi, 50% of Shimizu and 65% of Kofu with incendiaries. The Maruzen oil refinery at Wakayama is also hit with 500 lb. high explosive bombs. Only one B-29 is lost while attacking Shimizu.

Continuing its unrelenting incendiary attacks, the 20th Air Force, in the form of 475 B-29's, attack increasing numbers of urban areas, razing to the ground 27% of Sendai, 44% of Sakai, 52.5% of Wakayama and 73% of Gifu. Sixty-one B-29's attack the Utsube oil refinery at Yokkaichi with high explosives but fail to inflict significant damage. Once again allied losses are few. One B-29 crashes into the sea off the coast of Moji City while on a mining exercise in the Shimonoseki Strait, killing 11, with the only survivor being captured and later executed. Reports about the loss vary, with a tail gunner on a B-29 ahead of them saying he saw them hit by night fighters and another report blaming flak.

On 11 July, 25 B-29's once again mined the Shimonoseki Strait and waters around Miyazu, Obama Island and, in the first B-29 mission into Korean territory, two aircraft mine the waters around Pusan and Najin.

There were no missions on the 4/5/7/8/10 of July.

We were not pleased that they were taking our engines away. Major Luther Jones was especially upset. What really upset us was that we were going to lose engines that we trusted and had faith in, not to mention they had seen us through some very tough times. That wasn't all though. When you live through the times we did, the insanity of war, the stress of never knowing whether today was your last day on earth, small things take on bigger significance. We tended toward disciplined regimens and routines, we would do things in the same way every mission, wear lucky clothes, use lucky lighters – we became superstitious. If we were surviving we were obviously doing things right and none of us wanted to change that. Major Jones would have lobbied God himself if he had thought it would help us keep our engines. The thought of them being ripped out of the City of Monroe was heartbreaking – I am sure we all felt an emptiness in the pit of our stomachs.

While our old gal was being assaulted, we rested, slept a lot and tried to forget that soon enough we would be back in the thick of things putting all our trust in a new set of untried engines. Nothing would be quite the same again.

Being superstitious was common among a lot of the military, but flyers seemed to be particularly that way. The names and nose art of aircraft were all meant to provide some luck. Aircraft were given names such as 'The Bad Penny' (as in a bad penny always turns up); 'Lucky Eleven' (a reference to the number in the crew); 'Number Seven' and 'Boomerang', which don't need an explanation. It is interesting to note that on one of the aircraft called Boomerang, an actual boomerang was carried on every flight and was kept at the front of the plane, because, after all, a boomerang always comes back. Every mission was carefully inscribed on it along with the date.

A psychologist called George Clare, who himself was a flyer with the 10th Bomb Group, said that crews needed to identify with their planes and endow them with superhuman capabilities. Herb and the rest of the crew talked to the City of Monroe as if she were an extension of themselves, or another member of the crew. The plane was one of the team, a buddy – after all, buddies don't let their team-mates down!

4th of July, 10:30 PM. Everybody on the island is firing their guns in the air: rifles, machine guns, 45 revolvers, etc. Boy are the paddle foot officers burned up. The sky looks like an X-Mas tree it is so lit up by tracers. Ha, let them worry, nothing bothers me, bothers me, nothing bothers, me, burp-burp-burp!

It's the 4th of July and we're celebrating the birth of our country, the good old U. S. of A. We spent the day wandering the base, as transportation was difficult to get hold of and there weren't too many places to visit anyway.

However, later in the day we managed to 'borrow' a jeep so we went down to Agana, which is the capitol of Guam, and visited the beaches at Tumon Bay where we gathered small seashells and looked at the sparkling blue ocean. Tumon Bay is a coral reef so we had to wear our GI shoes to protect our feet, but it sure was pretty.

We missed our plane so we spent some time helping the ground crew with her – as much as we were able to anyway. We also spent some time at 21st Bomber Command headquarters watching Japanese prisoners cleaning up the grounds around the aircraft. They were certainly impressed with the sheer size of the B-29's, and one of them, realizing that his guards were not watching at that moment, reached across and touched the plane, as if to confirm this monstrous beast was truly real.

We tried our hand at climbing the coconut trees to see if we could liberate a few, but it was a lot harder getting to the top than it looked – none of us made it! Coming down was even worse as the rough scales of the tree point up–one slip and we might have been singing an octave or two higher.

We spotted an animal, no bigger than a small goat, that was later identified as a deer. The other thing that we saw a lot of was frogs. There were so many of them they made the Mississippi River pale by comparison. I think even Mark Twain would have been impressed!

Later in the day everybody was shooting into the air with machine guns, rifles, automatic pistols and an array of other things such as tracers. The noise was incredible. The tracers lit up the sky like a massive Christmas tree. We could have easily thwarted a moderately sized invasion attempt with all the ammo that was spent that day.

The reference in my diary to 'paddle foot' officers, also known as "gravel agitators" refers to any non-flight or non-rated officer, because they were always on the ground, never in the air like us.

The last comment about nothing worrying me, and the burp-burp-burp reference, was all to do with keeping me alert, aware and relaxed. I used to make a noise that sounded a little like burping which was like a nervous tic; it helped to relieve my stress and the pent up nervous energy I continually experienced.

Our fears concerning the new engines were not unfounded as one of them let us down straightaway and we had to return to base. We were on a test mission and had dumped our bombs on the island of Rota when it failed. Once we got back to Guam we had to circle the landing strip until we burned off enough fuel, otherwise the weight of that fuel would have been too much for our landing gear and tires. I was just glad we weren't over Japan when it gave up because in that situation you start to make yourself a target for Japanese fighter pilots pretty quickly.

The ground crew replaced the engine but it wasn't boding well for the future.

Herb was known for making things happen as he always knew the right people and was always finding ways around problems. Two such problems were the lack of ice cream and alcohol on Guam. He made friends with the mess/Sgt., who along with others, built a still back in the jungle. They acquired raisins from the mess hall and made a fine "raisin-jack".

As for the ice cream, Herb got the mess boys to make it for him from powdered milk and whatever else could be used. He then stored it in the bomb bay of the City of Monroe during their missions, where the temperature dropped to below zero, and when they returned they had frozen ice cream. That was Yankee ingenuity at its best.

Interestingly, ice cream was quite a big thing with the armed forces. The U.S. Navy commissioned a concrete oil barge in 1945 to act as a floating ice cream parlor. It cost them approximately $1 million and produced around 1,500 gallons of ice cream an hour. It had no engine and was towed around by tugs or any other ship that happened to be handy when it needed to be moved.

12 July, 1945

Five hundred and six bombers took part in five missions, and three B-29's were lost: one en route to the target, one en route to base and the third whereabouts unknown. One of the five missions used 500-pound general-purpose bombs and the rest incendiaries. Herb's bomb wing attacked the urban area of Uwajima and destroyed 14 square miles or some 14% of the city. Other wings hit Utsunomiya, razing to the ground some 34.2% of the city; Tsuruga had 68% of the urban area burnt out and finally just under 1% of Ichinomiya City was destroyed.

Herb's brother Don arrived in Guam in mid-July but Herb was unaware of his arrival. Don was assigned to the 29th Bomb Group as the co-pilot of a B-29 flying off North Field, the same airfield as Herb. It wasn't until some time later that their paths crossed.

In the fifth mission, high explosives tore apart the Kawasaki Petroleum Complex, destroying approximately 25% of the plant.

Mission #15, Target: Uwajima. July 12, 1945. Bomb load 40 each 500-pound incendiary bombs, flying time 14 hours 30 minutes. Target had 10/10 cover, under-cast bombed by radar. Trip to target was good except for one instance when we had a ship pass over us, not much over 10 feet above our tail. Kind of gave everyone a scare. Soup....we had 3 weather fronts between Guam and the target. Had a slightly rough time over the target. Some planes above us almost dropped them right in the middle of us. Return trip was okay, only awful tiresome.

At last we were finally back on the job and I know it sounds crazy, but the waiting was worse than anything. Although going on a mission was dangerous and really scary, not going on them meant you were hanging around in Guam, not working your way through the 32 missions you had to complete before you could go home.

Before we left we had a turkey dinner, or at least that's what they told us it was. It could well have been pigeon, but it was hot and there was plenty of it; that's all we cared about. It was an early dinner as our scheduled take-off time was 4:45pm. The briefing warned us of a weather front coming in but it was not thought to be severe. Pretty standard stuff for our first mission with the new engines.

Our target was Uwajima on the southeast side of Shikoku Island, and we were carrying AN-M47A2, 100# incendiary bombs with instantaneous nose detonation and E-46 500# incendiary clusters with the tail set to open 5,000 feet above target.

We completed our preflight checks, patted our lady and climbed aboard. The rituals continued inside the aircraft while I organized my coding and decoding books and settled down for a most welcome cigarette and cup of coffee.

It wasn't long before Major Jones announced that we were approaching the weather front but we all had a great deal of faith in Lt. Landregan's ability to steer us clear of the worst of the thunderheads and out of harm's way. In the end we didn't hit the front we had been briefed on, but found two different ones. This was a factor in why some planes made it to the target quicker than others did. Some were just better at finding their way through the bad weather.

After wandering around the maze of weather for awhile we approached our assembly point and found the front we had been briefed about.

We started to form up with other aircraft and proceeded to the Initial Point and then on to the target. By the time we got there the weather was 10/10 with solid cloud.

There were aircraft all over the sky. The weather was really tough, and we were fighting the wind and poor visibility. Major Jones told us that there were bombs dropping all around from our own planes. It was frightening, to think that there could be planes above us actually raining bombs down on us. It was then that I heard a plane above us, directly above us, close – too close. I looked out through the astrodome and boy, it was close all right! I could see the rivets on the underside of the plane as it crossed over us. It was rare for this to happen, but from time to time there were some near misses, and occasionally it wasn't a miss. We heard of one aircraft that was the victim of friendly bombs, if that isn't an oxymoron.

It was rare to hit three weather fronts in one trip. Even on the way back we had to maneuver around more thunderheads.

As the City of Monroe flew through thick cloud cover, one among 123 B-29's dropping, and in some cases dodging, some two million pounds of incendiary bombs, the tension was high. Herb, monitoring the radio, unable to do anything but sit and hope, put all his trust in the rest of the crew. In his own words he was scared half to death and emotionally exhausted, but it was all in a night's work.

13 July – 18 July, 1945

There was a mining mission on 13 July, but no missions flew on 14/16 of July. On the 15th there was a mining mission and one bombing mission targeting the Nippon Oil Company at Kudamatsu. The plant was almost entirely destroyed. On 16 July, Herb's one year wedding anniversary, there were four incendiary missions, involving 466 B-29's, 129 of them from Herb's bomb wing. No losses were reported. Twenty-seven B-29's mine the Shimonoseki strait and surrounding waters on 17 July; the following day is another quiet day with no missions leaving Guam.

Today was my one-year wedding anniversary and I wished like hell that I could see my wife. I missed her terribly and hoped she was doing okay. What a hell of a place to be on your 1st wedding anniversary, some 10,000 + miles away from the person you love. The thing about it was it wasn't just me, but every guy in Guam had important dates they were missing that were very personal and special to them, but not a damn thing any of us could do about it. It was always the special days that were the most demoralizing.

19 July, 1945

The City of Monroe is back in the air taking part in a mission with 125 other B-29's to drop 850 tons of incendiary bombs on the Okazaki urban area. They do a good job and destroy 68% of the city. Other bomb wings attack and destroy 84.5% the Fukui urban area, 64.5% of Hitachi and 33.5% of Choshi.

Eighty-three B-29's with the 315th Bomb Wing drop general purpose bombs on the Nippon Oil complex at Amagasaki, destroying 12 of the 14 buildings and leaving only a few oil tanks left undamaged.

Four B-29's are lost, resulting in eleven being killed in action, 23 missing in action, and eleven survivors, five of whom were captured and held as prisoners of war. Unlike many other B-29 crew members all five survived their ordeal and were returned to the U.S. after the war.

Mission #16, July 19, target: Okasaki, Honshu, raid was good. Big fire started in target area. Bomb load 184 each 100-pound gelatin bombs. Trip to and from target was unusually rough due to bad weather. And to my knowledge no ship went down. The attack by one plane would send a stream of tracers past our ship. They didn't miss us by more than 20 foot. The ship was flying a collision course with us. We dove and he dove. We saw he was going to hit us, so we pulled up very steep and climbed like hell...and he fired from not over a 100 yards out. We returned the fire and he went over us not more than 100 feet away. I was

sure wondering about things for awhile. They claimed it was a
B-29 from our group that fired upon us and we fired back, but I
still think it was a plane that had been shot down and was being
used by the Japs. He came in at us at about 3:00 o'clock with
identification lights on. And we could not identify him until he
started firing on us, and then we saw it to be a B-29 from the
long flash of flame coming out of the guns. I was riding in the
astrodome position and had seen it. Not a nice thing to be doing
miles from nowhere.

The diary entry above makes for scary reading. Herb and the crew of the
City of Monroe were fighting for their life against an enemy they could
hardly see. Imagine how they felt when it started to look as if one of their
own was attacking them.

The issue of friendly fire has been in the news a great deal in recent years
and it certainly happened from time to time during the Pacific War.
On 19 July, 1945 Herb was part of one such incident. To this day no one is
sure exactly what happened or who was at fault.

At the mission debrief it was revealed that the crew of the City of Monroe
had tracked the plane from a long way out because it had its lights on and
was heading for them. American aircraft never flew with their lights on
from the initial point (IP) through the target and back to the withdrawal
point (WP), however Japanese pilots did. Other pilots in Herb's group
had seen the plane's green and red recognition lights, including the one
on the tail. This wasn't the first time Japanese fighters had followed Herb's
plane with their lights on, so they didn't think too much of it at first. It
would not be impossible for the Japanese to repair and use an American
downed B-29, so even if the crew had realized it was a B-29, once it
started to fire on them they would have taken appropriate action.

*Major Jones maintained current power settings. This minimized the chance
of sparks coming from the turbos of the engines, which could reveal our
position. Of course, all our lights were out.*

Then, in an instant, things became a whole lot more serious. The unidentified plane fired on the City of Monroe, red hot flashes bursting from the muzzle of the plane's guns and it was only going to be a matter of seconds before the hot metal would come screaming through the fragile hull and the even more fragile bodies of its occupants.

After we were fired upon we returned fire. This was not only human instinct, but was a major point of emphasis during gunnery school. We were told "if fire is iniated then return fire is warranted" unless of course, you were suicidal. As he came closer we saw the high dorsal fin of the bomber and the turret gun, and Tim called back from the front and told Buck to quit shooting as our new enemy has been identified as another B-29. Once we stopped firing the other plane disappeared and we were once again alone in the sky. It was like it had never happened – as if the other plane had just been a phantom.

At the debriefing Herb and the rest of his crew discovered that a B-29 had been shot up over the withdrawal point and the tail gunner wounded. He was hospitalized on Iwo, while the rest of the crew had returned to Guam.

Buck told the investigators that the other B-29 had started firing first and that he had only responded to what he considered enemy fire. The attacking plane had come up at us nose-first traveling up the coastline. It was thought that it was either lost or had failed to get over its target and was returning to Guam at the time of the incident.

We assumed it was a Japanese fighter since all its lights were on, plus, of course, the fact that it was firing at us. At night and from that distance, we couldn't see its shape so we couldn't make out that it was a B-29.

Sometime later the plane was brought to Guam. It was shot up pretty bad with holes in its tail section. It was declared our gunner's fault and they took a stripe away from Buck. The other crew claimed they never fired on us, so it was their word against ours. Personally I think they cleaned their guns while they were in Iwo Jima, that way the investigators would not be able to tell whether they had been fired. The reason we were declared at fault was that we didn't have any holes to show for the altercation. I suppose we got shafted because we were better in a fight. At the end of the day somebody was lying, but I was never really sure who.

One thing for certain is that just because we were all on the same side didn't mean that everyone was honorable. Major Jones often commented that we had never passed over a target. We always managed to drop our bombs no matter how bad the weather, or how hard the enemy tried to stop us. We always stuck with it to the end, which was more than could be said for some of our fellow airmen. There were times when huge areas of the ocean were literally boiling where B-29's had dropped their bombs and hightailed it home.

T/Sgt & Right Gunner Joe Buck was married and was in his early 20's. Joe was one of the unfortunate soldiers who received a "Dear John" letter from his wife, stating she had found another. One can only imagine how he must have felt given this and the taking of a stripe due to the so-called 'Friendly Fire' situation.

24 July, 1945

Seven missions were flown involving 572 B-29's. The focus: Nagoya and Osaka. Targets included a propeller factory, three aircraft plants, an arsenal, and urban areas. The missions were highly successful with the factories being either partially or completely destroyed. The Kawanishi Aircraft plant was 77% destroyed along with the principal assembly buildings of the Nakajima plant. Only one B-29 was lost; shot down over Osaka Bay during the actual bombing. Ten members of the crew were killed and one was captured and later executed.

July 24 1945 Mission 17, target Handa (Honshu). Daylight raid, hit target about 1200 PM, Bomb load 30 ea 500 lb G.P. raid as far as we know was successful no fighter opposition very little flack, there was a heavy undercast when we hit target. Went in, in formation and lead ship messed up and we had to go around and make another run on target. We landed at Iwo Jima due to lowness of gasoline. There were about 200 ships beside us who landed at Iwo Jima, was about 600 B-29's in yesterday's raid.

The lead ship messed up. We were not sure why, it could have been pilot error or perhaps his radar wasn't working. The whole group had to go back to the initial point in formation. We did a 90° turn and started our run again.

This would have made this particular mission far more dangerous. The idea was to get in and get out as fast as possible. The more time spent in enemy territory the more likely it was that you would be shot down, so the lead ship would not have been popular on this occasion.

The first two squadrons of our Bomb Group missed the target, and the rest of the wing didn't do much better. Our squadron, the 62nd, was the exception. We made our bombing run on radar and were so accurate that our single squadron destroyed over 39% of the total roof area of the Nakajima plant.

It turned out that this raid was one of the best radar bombing runs in the history of B-29's in the Pacific.

The mess-up by the lead aircraft had left us short of fuel so we had to head for Iwo Jima to refuel. As we looked back toward Japan there was a series of ten to fifteen red flares. The flares indicated that there were wounded on board and the B-29's in question needed landing priority but we were all short of fuel so not all of us were lucky enough to make it back.

I remember this was an eerie feeling. You started to think about the men on those planes, injured, perhaps dying. Who were they, what were they like, did they have wives, girlfriends, children, brothers and sisters? Did they come from a large city or a small town? Had they ever thought, for even one minute, that this is where they might die? That their hopes and dreams would end in an aluminum tube, with Japanese shrapnel tearing their body apart?

As Herb watched those flares, so similar, but then again so deadly different, to fourth of July fireworks, it made him think of life in a way that he had never done before; in a way that no 23-year-old should ever have to.

25 July, 1945

The City of Monroe didn't fly on this day, but 75 B-29's bombed the Mitsubishi Oil and Hayama Petroleum Companies at Kawasaki. Thirty-three percent of their storage tanks and other facilities were destroyed. Another 25 planes took part in mining operations in Japanese and Korean waters.

One B-29 was picked out by searchlights on the approach to the target and hit by flak. It crashed into the Nippon Casting Company factory and all the crew were killed in action.

26 July, 1945

On this day, all flights were incendiary missions and Herb flew with 23 other B-29's from the 314th bomb wing and destroyed 2.1 square miles, or 38%, of the city of Omuta. One plane was lost from the 19th Bomb Group. It crashed in the woods near Yokoyama Village, Yame County, Fukuoka Prefecture. Two of the crew were killed in action, and one was killed by villagers as he resisted being taken into custody. The remaining eight were captured and taken to Seibu army headquarters where they were later executed.

Other bomb wings attacked Matsuyama, destroying 1.22 square miles, or 73%, of the city. They also bombed the urban area of Tokuyama, destroying almost a half-square mile, or 37%, of the city.

A total of 348 B-29's hit targets with just the one plane lost.

> July 26 1945. Mission 18, target Omuta. Night raid was good. Bomb load 20 each 500-pound incendiary bombs in front bay & 92 100-pound gasoline jelly bombs in rear bomb bay. No opposition seen. Three burst of flak. Flying time 15 hrs 40 min, fires were very good, spread out over a big area & solid smoke was observed up to 16,000 foot. Population 65,000 per square mile. Return was good.

We carried a mixture of bombs on this mission. The reason was almost certainly based on intelligence gathered about our target for that night. The intelligence officers would know what the buildings were made out of, whether they were built out of wood, metal, concrete or whatever.

Metal and concrete buildings, for instance, aren't affected by the jelly as much as by thermite, so it would depend on what the majority of buildings were made of as to what type of bombs we would drop.

The M60 thermite cluster bombs we dropped weighed 500 pounds each and looked like a large bundle of sticks banded together.

At this stage of the war the B-29's had run out of major targets as all the large cities had been pretty much destroyed, so the targets were becoming smaller and consisted of sites where it was known that manufacturing was taking place. Priority was given to those sites posing the greatest threat.

It is interesting to note the comment in Herb's diary for this day. He quietly states "population 65,000 per square mile". When you consider that on this mission alone Herb's bomb wing razed to the ground some 2.1 square miles of a city and somewhere in the region of 130,000 people were either killed, injured or lost their homes, you start to understand the destructive power of the raids. That was an awful lot to put on the shoulders of these young men. At 23 years of age, the fact that it was an entry in his diary at all showed that the result of this action was very much at the forefront of the young Herb's mind.

27 July, 1945

While Herb and his fellow crew members were on a rest day, a night mission to mine the Shimonoseki Strait at Fukuoka, Niigata, Maizuru, Sensaki and in Fukawa Bay by 24 B-29's suffered three losses due to heavy flak. Two of the aircraft were lost in enemy territory and one crash-landed on Iwo Jima. Of the two crews that crashed near or over Japan, one was forced to bail out 50 miles south of Shikoku Island. The survivors were picked up by the submarine USS Whale after spending two days afloat in life rafts. Five of the crew were killed in action. The other plane crashed in the Inland Sea, about a mile from Sada-Misaki, Ehime Prefecture. A Navy rescue plane, as was the case in the other casualty that night, rescued the survivors, and the other five crew members were killed in action.

The B-29 that did make it back to Iwo Jima was subsequently scrapped due to structural damage from the pounding of heavy flak bursts.

28 July, 1945

Herb was back in action on a night that saw seven missions flown, with 547 aircraft attacking Japan, amazingly without a single aircraft lost. The City of Monroe, in a mission involving just 29 aircraft, bombed the Uwajima urban area, destroying a little over half a square mile, accounting for 52% of the city. The 314th also hit the Ogaki area with 90 aircraft and destroyed .48 square miles or 40% of the city.

The other bomb wings on this busy night were equally successful over the Tsu urban area, destroying .84 square miles or 57% of the city area after seventy-six bombers visited. Sixty-one B-29's hit the Aomori urban area, destroying a little over one square mile or 64% of the city area; one hundred and twenty two aircraft attacked Ichinomiya, destroying just under one square mile, or 37%, of the city; ninety-three Superfortresses attacked Uji-Yamada razing to the ground 39% of the city, an area of .36 square miles; and seventy-six of these formidable aircraft, using high explosives, bombed the Shimotsu Oil Refinery, taking out 75% of the tank capacity, and 90% of the gasometer capacity. Sixty-nine percent of the roof area was also destroyed or damaged.

The destruction continued night after night and still Japan would not surrender. The dominance of the B-29 was at this point almost complete. The ability to fly seven missions over enemy territory, utilizing 547 aircraft and experience no casualties speaks for itself.

July 29, 45 Mission 19, target Ogaki (Honshu). Bomb load 20 each 500-lb incendiary 92 100-lb gas jelly. Japs were pre-warned & had dummy fires started all over the place. Command had a ship from 330th Bomb Group, named City of Omaha, with news commentators on board broadcasting to the States as they went over the target. We were less than forty miles behind him as he was broadcasting from the I.P. into the target. The dummy fires confused some of the crews but we were lucky and didn't have any trouble. Flak was meager, few searchlights in area. Mission was good.

We didn't drop just any type of bomb; our armaments were decided based on the construction materials used to build our target cities. On this mission we would be dropping 500lb thermite clusters which had an explosive in the center of the bomb and a tail which set off a charge at a preset altitude. This meant we had to maintain our briefed altitude over the target. This was a further demonstration of the importance of sticking to each and every facet of a mission. Any deviation could compromise the mission and dramatically increase the chance of colliding with another aircraft, resulting in the certain death of both crews.

Herb and the crew faced many dangers during a mission. Mechanical failure could mean ditching into an angry sea hundreds of miles from land, quite possibly in enemy territory. Weather was a constant concern. Head winds and crosswinds consumed precious fuel as the pilot increased power to maintain the aircraft's briefed position in the bomber stream.

The term "bomber stream" was used to describe the hundreds of bombers flying one behind the other, either on their way to the target or returning after a raid; this was referred to as 'in trail'. The B-29's were spaced ten to fifteen miles apart and were required to maintain a specific altitude. Imagine, 800 or more aircraft each 100 feet long leaving from Saipan, Tinian and Guam, all merging together at a predetermined spot while at the same time keeping a ten-mile distance from each other, all at a briefed altitude. Keeping over 120 miles of aircraft in a bomber stream and preventing them from hitting each other, is a critical and delicate business. As you can imagine, one small deviation and the results could be catastrophic.

This was especially dangerous at night, or during bad weather. Even though running lights were allowed for part of the journey, they often could not see, or be seen, by other aircraft.

Aircraft were permitted to use their running lights only until they reached a predetermined number of miles from the Initial Point (IP). They would then proceed, blacked-out, to the target and beyond until they reached their Withdrawal Point (WP) before continuing on a heading back toward their home base.

To further complicate the lives of these brave airmen, they invariably had to fly their aircraft through a minimum of one, sometimes two and as many as three weather fronts, usually between Iwo and mainland Japan. This dramatically increased the potential for air to air collisions, due to lack of visibility, and the danger of running into heavy thunderheads was always present. The latter resulted in winds that could tear an aircraft to pieces as if it were a papier-mâché piñata.

Now, try to imagine performing this feat of airmanship in a crowded sky of 300 or more other huge bombers while flak is exploding all around you and the thermals from the firestorms below are trying their best to rocket you hundreds, if not thousands, of feet skyward!

Tonight the people of Japan were expecting us, especially those in the cities, where thousands of leaflets had previously been dropped warning the Japanese people of possible attack.

The leaflet Herb talks about identified the cities on a particular mission and warned citizens to evacuate. Printed in Japanese it translated into English as follows:

Read this carefully as it may save your life or the life of a relative or friend. In the next few days, the military installations in four or more of the cities named on the reverse side of this leaflet will be destroyed by American bombs.

These cities contain military installations and workshops of factories which produce military goods. We are determined to destroy all the tools of the military clique which they are using to prolong this useless war. But, unfortunately, bombs have no eyes, so in accordance with American well known humanitarian principles, the American Air Force which does not wish to injure innocent people, now gives you warning to evacuate the cities named and save your lives.

America is not fighting the Japanese people but is fighting the military group that has enslaved the Japanese people.

The peace, which America will bring, will free the people from the oppression of the military and mean the emergence of a new and better Japan.

You can restore peace by demanding new and good leaders who will end the war.

We cannot promise that only these cities will be among those attacked but at least four will be, so heed this warning and evacuate these cities.

The list of doomed cities that was printed on the opposite side of the leaflet were Admori, Nishinomiya, Ogaki, Kurume, Ichinomiya, Nagnika, Koriyama, Kakodate, Ujiyamada, and Tsu. The cities which were bombed were Admori, Ichinomiya, Ujiyamada and Ogaki (which the City of Monroe participated in).

The leaflets were used to both notify the Japanese people of America's intent and to reduce the loss of innocent Japanese lives.

It is ironic that 60 years later, the leaflets dropped by our military in Iraq and Afghanistan are strikingly similar to those used in World War II. It seems the countries change, but not the message.

By the time we got there everything had been shut down and the towns were quiet. Given the warning, many people may have taken heed of the leaflets and evacuated. Once over our target we could see dummy fires which had been purposely set to confuse us into thinking it was a target identifier hit by one of our pathfinder aircraft outlining the target parameters. It had little effect on the outcome as massive areas of the city were destroyed.

Our crew didn't have any trouble telling the dummy fires from the real thing as a couple of aircraft ahead of us had already bombed the target and called us on the radio and told us where they were. With their help and guidance we dropped our bombs precisely on the area as briefed. We were mighty thankful as this not only made us a great deal more accurate but made the entire bomb run a lot safer as well! This was an excellent example of the type of results that can be attained when not only are the individuals in each crew working well together, but also, extending that philosophy, all aircraft worked as a team.

THE END
IS NEAR
(AUGUST 1945)

CHAPTER NINE

When faith is lost, when honor dies, the man is dead!
—Whittier

21,029 tons of bombs dropped

8,438 tons High Explosive; 12,591 tons Incendiary

3,331 sorties, 3,145 effective[8]

MISSION #20 TARGET KAWASAKI (HONSHU)
AUGUST 1 1945 NITE RAID
We went as a RCM ship had
a lot of radar jamming equipment
aboard we carried one bomb bay
tank and no bombs. Our Job was
to circle over the target for an
hr + 20 minutes and jam the
the Jap search lights, radar anti-
aircraft guns and radar equipt

[8] http://www.ww2guide.com/b29ops.shtml

NEWS

Major General Curtis E. LeMay, whose idea it was to have B-29's carry out low-level incendiary raids on Japan, is promoted to Chief of Staff under General Carl Spaatz, Commander of Strategic Air Forces in the Pacific. The B-29 crews get a new commander. Nathan F. Twining, previously commander of the thirteenth and fifteenth Air Forces, takes over from LeMay. Fresh from Europe, Twining had been commander of the Mediterranean Allied Strategic Air Forces and at 48 was a veteran who had experienced being forced down at sea, spending six days adrift in the South Pacific earlier in his career. Although not as charismatic a figure as LeMay, he was well qualified to take over his sterling work.

By this time the 20th Air Force was completely dominant over Japan. William H. Lawrence of the New York Times reported from a B-29 in August, 1945 that "Japanese resistance is so meager as to be almost unbelievable." He went on to say that there was little anti-aircraft fire and few enemy night fighters, and commented on the fact that even though the enemy knew 24 hours in advance the attack was coming, they could do nothing to save the harbor city of Aomori from being burnt to the ground.

The skies above Japan were, by this time, constantly full of U.S. aircraft that were able to pretty much come and go as they pleased.

August saw a number of war movies showing at theaters across the U.S. "Anchors Aweigh" saw Frank Sinatra, Gene Kelly and Kathryn Grayson sing and dance their way through this long movie about two sailors on liberty in Los Angeles; and "Story of G.I. Joe" starring Robert Mitchum and Burgess Meredith was a human interest war story about company 'C' of the 18th infantry fighting its way across North Africa, told from the perspective of a war correspondent.

2 August, 1945

Over 800 B-29's attacked Japan on this night. If the Japanese thought the United States would ease off now that the major cities had been destroyed then they were sadly mistaken. Thirty-seven planes mined their shipping lanes, 169 attacked Hachioji, destroying 80% of the city, and another 173 destroyed Toyama almost entirely, wiping out its aluminum, ball bearing and special steel production facilities in the process. One hundred twenty-five B-29's hit Nagaoka, razing to the ground more than 65% of the city, while an additional 125 bombed the Mitsubishi Oil Company at Kawasaki, causing further damage to that inflicted in earlier raids.

Herb's wing, 160 of them, bombed Mito and destroyed 65% of the city.

Amazingly, once again there was only one aircraft lost, while bombing Hachioji. Out of twelve crew members, one was killed in action, one was killed while resisting capture and the remaining ten survived a stay in the Ofuna prisoner of war camp.

Mission #20, target: Kawasaki, August 2 1945 night raid (Honshu). We went as a RCM ship, had a lot of radar jamming equipment aboard. We carried one bomb bay tank and no bombs. Our job was to circle over the target for an hour and 20 minutes and jam the Jap searchlights, radar, anti-aircraft guns, and radar equipment; night fighters in the area.

I sat in the astrodome all the time over the target. It was a very effective raid, and the Japs had been warned the night before that we were coming. We saw about 45 searchlights and about five night fighters. Although there were more in the vicinity. We were flying at 19,500-feet. Lights out and circling the target area. What was so funny about it is that Kawasaki is between Tokyo and Yokohoma. We were flying a circular course that took us directly across the center of Yokohoma out into Tokyo Bay then around and across the center of Tokyo then around and followed same course again for three times. Seen some night fighters fire at B-29's, but don't know if they were hit. We could see the tracers stream by them. They caught quite a few B-29's in the searchlights, and flak was bursting all around them, some close. One 29 was hit on #3 engine by flak and caught fire, he got it out I guess, because he did not use emergency radio.

We also observed flak at our level, meager though and not too accurate. Our target was petroleum storage tanks. The area was dark and when some of those tanks blew they lit up the whole area. We could even see Mount Fuji as plain as day. Raid was good and very big fires were started. Do not know our losses. We returned without mishap.

That night we came in higher than the others did, a lot higher. We were at 20,000 feet looking down at the rest who were at 8,000. Our job was to jam enemy radar. The mission itself called for a low level night raid. The Japanese radar would lock-on to our boys' aircraft with their guns and then follow them, firing continuously. By activating the jammers we confused and neutralized their radar. This worked for searchlights as well.

We circled over the center of Yokohama and then out and back around Tokyo Bay, passing close to Kawasaki. It was fascinating, circling and watching the drama unfold beneath us. It was funny to have balcony seats at a show at which we usually center stage performers.

We were a bit like sitting ducks as the Japanese possessed guns that could reach us even at 20,000 feet, but our two radar operators did a great job at jamming their equipment. The Japs did get some lock-ons but very few were effective.

One of the things I remember most about that mission was the site of Mount Fuji, in what should have been the darkness of night, shining brightly forty miles away, lit up in a way that only 800 or so B-29's can achieve.

5 August, 1945

Back in action, Herb's crew flew their 24th mission (if we include the three Rota training missions) alongside 249 other aircraft from the 73rd and 314th bomb wings and bombed Nishinomiya-Mikage, destroying almost 30% of the city. One B-29 was lost on this mission, but all the crew survived.

Once again B-29's were busy mining Japanese waters, while 219 aircraft from other bomb wings rained incendiary bombs down on the urban areas of Saga, Maebashi and Imabari, losing one crew over Saga.

One hundred and six B-29's completely destroyed the Ube Coal Liquefaction Company factory in Ube using high explosives.

August 5, 1945 Mission #21, (Honshu). Target: Kobe and Osaka urban areas between Osaka and Kobe. Raid was night raid, we carried 40 each 500-lb. incendiary clusters and one photo flash bomb.

On our bomb run we had ships passing over us, and you could just barely see them in the dark. We made our bomb run at 12,800 feet, there were very big fires and smoke was up to 20,000 feet. Smoke was very thick and black and stench was terrible at our altitude.

The smoke cloud at the top was about 4 miles wide and solid. After we passed over the target we saw two fighters, but they never saw us so they didn't bother us. There was about ten searchlights and about 12 to 25 heavy guns which were sending up plenty, also a lot of automatic weapons fire which did not get up to our altitude.

Some air-to-air bombing was going on, and some of the fighters were firing rockets. We were over the mainland about 45 minutes, left the mainland and returned to base without any trouble. Had a radar tracking fighter on our tail for awhile, but finely shook him. To my knowledge no ships were lost. The people at this target were warned that we were coming.

We were lead ship on this mission and dropped a 120-pound photo-flash bomb by parachute. The photo-flash illuminated at 1 million-candle power and lit up the whole area and helped the bombardiers to identify the target clearly. Visibility was low that night even with the help of the photo-flash bomb. The other thing I remember, even though it was 60 years ago, was the remarkable stench that rose from the ground. It worked its way, like a living thing, through every part of the aircraft - the smell of burning human flesh.

It is hard to imagine what Herb and the rest of the crew of the City of Monroe were feeling on that summer night. They were on their 21st mission, veterans in terms of combat, but still more than anything, they were young men living through terrible times. To be locked away in an aluminum tube thousands of feet above such total destruction, unable to escape the smell of death and the thought that so many human souls were permeating their very bodies must have been horrifying. How many of us today could face such a situation?

As soon as we dropped our bombs the anti-aircraft fire found us. We immediately climbed higher trying to get out of range; we changed course, then tried to dive into the darkness. If they couldn't see us they couldn't hit us, all the time the smell of death following us.

As Herb sat there at his station, the pilot was trying everything to get them to safety. To make matters worse, the anti-aircraft guns below were firing shells containing phosphorus. The idea was to fire above the formation and have the shells explode at a set altitude in an umbrella fashion. Their success was dependent on whether Japanese radar was accurate with regards to the altitude and airspeed of the B-29 formation.

Phosphorus when it rained down from above could burn its way through the skin of an aircraft like a hot knife through butter. Anything, or anyone in its path would suffer extreme burns, as phosphorus continues to burn, even embedded in flesh or metal without oxygen, until it disappears. It can burn right through flesh to the bone. It is almost colorless, wax like, sometimes with a yellowish tinge to it, and smells like garlic. It's nickname Willy Pete (**W**hite **P**hosphorus) belies its evil nature. This is just another example of the multiplicity of dangers faced by these young men who fought for our freedom.

They were firing rockets at us too, but they weren't too accurate with them. By today's standards they were like Roman Candles, but still plenty scary when they're zipping past you.

6 August, 1945

Some time after 08:00 am the City of Monroe was nearing its return to Guam from the previous night's Kobe, Osaka mission. Herb, close to home and safe after another successful mission, relaxed at his radio operator station. All of a sudden he felt a cold chill, just for a brief moment. It passed through his body and then left as quickly as it had

come. He shrugged it off and thought no more about it, that is, until
he landed.

*Once landed, we proceeded to debriefing and were immediately informed
of a sole B-29, the Enola Gay, which had just made history. I immediately
thought of the weird feeling that I had experienced earlier that morning.*

At precisely 08:15 am (the bomb exploded at 08:16:02 Hiroshima
time) Colonel Paul Tibbets, the pilot of the Enola Gay, was flying over
Hiroshima, one of Japan's main supply depots for the army, and dropped
a new weapon on the unsuspecting people below.

It was the most powerful bomb anyone had ever used and was set to
change the course of the war. Two B-29's accompanied the Enola Gay as
observers. They were not told of the exact nature of their mission, but
were issued instructions that if a rescue attempt was needed they were
to wait thirty minutes before proceeding. They were approximately fifty
miles from the detonation.

The Hiroshima Atomic Bomb, 20,000 tons of TNT in the initial blast
(equal to a 13,000 tons or a 13 kiloton TNT explosion, as a result of the
chain reaction) was dropped from a height of 31,060 feet, parachuted
down toward earth and exploded 50 seconds later at a height of 1,850
feet, a mere 550 feet from its target, the Aioi bridge.

Colonel Tibbets later talked about a bright light filling the plane and
an awful mushroom cloud. The co-pilot Lewis pounded on Tibbets'
shoulder, exclaiming, "Look at that! Look at that! Look at that!" He said
the atomic fission tasted like lead. Then he asked himself "My God, what
have we done?"

A new era of warfare was announced by an explosion and flash of light
followed immediately by a heat wave of staggering proportions; 7,000
degrees Fahrenheit of death burnt everything in its path, driven by a wind
five times greater than a strong hurricane. Even one mile from the site
of the explosion the wind was strong enough to destroy brick buildings.
Accounts vary, but approximately 80% of the buildings in Hiroshima
were destroyed. An estimated 71,000 people were killed in the blast and

by the end of the year 140,000 had perished. In total, due to the long-term effects of radiation, 200,000 people died from the dropping of this single bomb on a single city.

And yet, President Truman would say that it was not the most devastating air attack of the war. The March fire raids on Tokyo had a greater effect, he said. That may be so in terms of destruction and even loss of life, but the sheer power of Little Boy, the nickname of the bomb (named for President Roosevelt) made it a symbol that sixty years later still has the power to bring fear into the hearts of us all. Weapons of mass destruction are a major concern today; in the wrong hands they would have a devastating effect on world peace. In 1945, at great cost, they brought about peace. The next time they are used it may be a different story.

The President stated, "If they do not now accept our terms they may expect a rain of ruin from the air the like of which has never been seen on Earth. Behind this air attack will follow by sea and land, forces in such number and power as they have not yet seen, but with fighting skill of which they are already aware."

The terms he was referring to were the Potsdam Declaration of July 26, which was a statement issued by Harry S. Truman, Winston Churchill and General Chiang Kai-Seek of China that outlined the terms of surrender for Japan as agreed at the Potsdam conference.

8, August 1945

At Guam it was back to normal the day after the atomic bomb had been dropped on Hiroshima. There was no let up for the B-29 crews or the Japanese people. Although Herb and the City of Monroe weren't active, 381 B-29's flew three missions, two during the day and one during the night. Seven aircraft were lost, resulting in the last loss of B-29 crews during the war.

Yawata was hit with incendiaries destroying 21% of the city. During this mission a B-29 is shot down and three more are lost due to mechanical failure. Like the crews, the aircraft are beginning to get tired.

The second mission of the day hit Tokyo once again with 60 aircraft, the target being an aircraft plant and an arsenal. Once again B-29's are lost, two to flak and one to mechanical failure.

On the last mission that night, 91 B-29's attack Fukuyama with incendiaries, destroying over 73% of the city.

One of the crews from the 'Nip Clipper', was badly shot up over the target, but managed to make it to open sea where the crew bailed out. All survived except for the commander, who waited until all his crew were safe before he attempted to leave the aircraft, by which time he was no longer able to do so. The crew drifted in a life raft for a week before being picked up by the enemy. They were taken to just outside Hiroshima by truck, and then lined up on their knees. The Japanese Colonel ordered them to be beheaded, but a Lieutenant advised him against it, as it would constitute a war crime. This apparently worked and the men of the 'Nip Clipper' were taken to a POW camp and lived to tell the tale. [9]

9 August, 1945

Three million leaflets were dropped on Japanese towns warning them that more atomic bombs would be dropped if their government did not unconditionally surrender.

Three days had passed and the Japanese had still not surrendered, so President Truman ordered a second atomic bomb dropped. This time Kokura Arsenal on Kyushu Island was the target, and the bomb was a whole lot bigger. Nicknamed 'Fat Man' after Winston Churchill, the British Prime Minister, it weighed in at an enormous 9,000lbs with the power of 20 kilotons of TNT.

Fat Man was dropped by the B-29 Bockscar, flown by Major Charles Sweeney, commanding officer of the 393rd squadron, and his regular crew from the B-29 Great Artiste. The crews of Bockscar and Great Artiste swapped aircraft for this mission so Capt. Fred Bock flew the Great Artiste, which had been the observer plane on the Hiroshima flight, and still had onboard all the equipment needed to measure the effects of an atomic explosion.

Bad weather over the Kokura Arsenal on Kyushu Island caused a change of plan and Nagasaki, home of the Mitsubishi Torpedo factory, became the new target for this second wave of death and destruction, aimed at making Japan finally sit up and take notice.

[9] Thanks to Earl Johnson for this story which he heard at a reunion of the 9th Group, told he thinks by the Navigator. http://home.att.net/~sallyann6/b29/56years-4508a.html

At 11:02a.m. the bomb Fat Man was dropped over Nagasaki at 28,900 feet and exploded 1,625 feet above the ground, after falling silently for almost a minute. Approximately 74,000 people were killed and another 70,000 were injured. The bomb destroyed 6.7 million square meters of the city and destroyed, or badly damaged, some 18,500 buildings and/or homes.

Aircraft returning home from other missions reported seeing smoke at 50,000 feet.

Although Fat Man was a larger bomb, it caused fewer deaths, as Nagasaki is surrounded by mountains, which contained the damage.

The two bombs were actually different, not just in size but also in how they were fuelled. Little Boy contained highly enriched Uranium-235 while Fat Man had a Plutonium core surrounded by high explosives. In terms of destruction however, the difference was, to the people on the ground, a moot point.

On Guam, missions are still operating as normal and 95 B-29's bomb the oil refinery at Armagasaki. At this point Japan is on its knees. Attacks of such incredible severity have it reeling.

10 August, 1945

The Japanese government announces that it wants peace. On Guam, orders are to limit operations to precision missions.

Seventy B-29's leave Guam and pick up two groups of P-51s at Iwo Jima as escorts to Tokyo. If the Japanese think there might be some respite they are wrong. Mining of Japanese waters also continues apace as 31 B-29's are hard at work during the night.

Mission #22, Target: Tokyo (Honshu). Nakajima aircraft plant 8-10-45, bomb load 4 each 2,000-pound general purpose: demolition bombs, target was clear. Went in on bomb run a 24,500-feet.

Were flying along and taking best evasive action we could and still fly formation when everything was nice and quiet, not much conversation on interphone, when all of a sudden we hear a hell of an explosion and the airplane jumped about 200 feet up in the air and slid sideways, kind of wobbly. After checking the airplane we found about four-foot hole in the left wing and a few holes in the side of the fuselage and tail.

We left formation and headed from the center of Tokyo towards Tokyo Bay to get out of there. We got some more flack off the Tokyo area, but wasn't too accurate. We finally got out to sea and headed for Iwo Jima figuring on landing there but didn't have to the plane was still flying ok.

When we landed at Guam we only had about 400 gallons of gas left, but we made it. When we finished counting we had 53 holes in the airplane besides the large one which was big enough to drop a man through. No one was hurt.

In advance of an unconditional surrender Herb is still flying and sets off on what will be his last bombing mission of the war; and what a mission it turns out to be! Seventy B-29's set off to bomb an arsenal at the Nakajima aircraft factory. The arsenal was underground so the City of Monroe wasn't carrying its normal 500-pound high explosive bombs for this type of precision bomb run, but four massive 2,000-pound bombs with delayed action fuses that would bury themselves into the earth and destroy underground chambers.

When the explosion hit the wing all hell let loose. The first thing we heard was Jones yelling, "what in the hell is going on back there?" Tommy the ring gunner could see the hole. He reported back, "It's okay Major, we've been hit but we look alright." He may have been a little optimistic, at that point, as the ailerons wouldn't move and Jones had to fly on trim tab alone. Not so good when you are over enemy territory.

When Major Jones noted that the control wheel wouldn't move he immediately grabbed the trim tab control and used it to maintain normal flight. If he hadn't been such a highly experienced pilot he might well have panicked at the shock of being hit, and lost control. As it was he immediately evaluated the situation and prevented the aircraft from spinning out of control and falling from the sky. Had the City of Monroe been in any degree of bank when we were hit, we may not have been able to recover, regardless of Jones' superior flying skills.

The hole was about five feet out, towards the wing tip and approximately eight feet from the outboard fuel tank called the 'Tokyo Tank'. It was times like this that you thought about how close you were to being just another 'killed in action' statistic.

All our hard work, training, preparation and experience would have meant nothing if we had been hit close to or directly on that tank just eight feet from the gaping hole. The explosion would have killed us all. On this day those few feet separated living and dying.

Once we had left the bay on the main island of Honshu, we were cruising at a little over 20,000 feet and things were getting real tense. Our aircraft had taken a battering, but at least it was still flying. One of our more serious problems was that our ailerons were locked, so we had to fly strictly on trim tabs. I received a call on the interphone from Major Jones; he told me to call the ground station at Iwo Jima and report our condition. Once Iwo had received my message, they challenged me with the code of the day, which I then provided. Aircraft were forbidden to fly over Iwo above 10,000 feet, so I had to request authorization to cross at 23,000 feet where the air resistance was lower and we would use less fuel.

We really wanted to make it back to home base for repairs – it was a matter of pride.

Iwo gave us permission to cross at 23,000 feet; they did have reservations however, and sent up two P-51's and two P-47's to check out whether we were who we said we were. I for one was mighty glad to see these fighters on our wing tips, and the sight of the pilots giving us the old high sign and rocking their wings up and down in the time-honored sign of recognition in the aviation world, filled me with hope, pride and camaraderie.

We managed to get to within sight of Guam without any further problems. Then Jones addressed the whole crew by interphone, saying, "Boys, you can leave this thing now, if you choose, I'll take her in." Given the difficulty he was having maintaining normal flight and the major doubts surrounding our ability to land we had all been offered the opportunity to bail out. With the ship handling like a sack of potatoes, and no guarantees he would bring her down safely, he wanted to make sure we all made it out okay. None of us knew how bad the landing would be, but we were sure of one thing, "that we were all in this together and there was no way any of us were leaving".

We came in over Guam praying that we wouldn't fly straight into the cliff. As we maneuvered lower and lower the ground seemed to approach abnormally fast. My mouth was dry and I am sure I wasn't the only one feeling scared. We shouldn't have worried though, Major Jones was one of the best damn pilots around and he put the old girl down as sweetly as if she had been fancying her flight to a crowd of dignitaries below.

It turned out that the aircraft had 54 holes in it, including the one that was larger than any one of the crew!

The wing had to be replaced from the engine out, but without the superior flying skills of Major Jones, the 20th Air Force might have lost another Superfortress and its valuable cargo.

Herb had completed 23 missions and the United States had dropped the ultimate weapon, twice, and it seemed that still the Japanese were not giving up; in fact, for Herb, things seemed to be heating up. This mission *was* very nearly his last.

14 August, 1945

Japanese surrender may have been imminent, but you wouldn't have known it on Guam as 752 B-29's thundered down the runways, flying seven missions without loss. A naval arsenal was bombed at Hikari, an army arsenal at Osaka, and railroad yards at Marifu. In the longest non-stop mission by B-29's, 132 aircraft bomb the Nippon Oil Company at Tsuchizakiminato, a round trip of 3,650 miles. The Kumagaya urban area was hit with incendiaries and 45% of the city was destroyed. Seventeen percent of the Isezaki urban area was destroyed by incendiaries, and B-29's tirelessly continued to mine Japanese waters.

These were to be the last bombing missions of the war as President Truman announced the unconditional surrender of Japan before the final B-29's returned to their bases. Although Herb and the crew of the City of Monroe didn't get to take part in this last attack on the enemy, the excitement was far from over.

Herb and his crew were grounded as the City of Monroe underwent significant repairs to replace a major part of the wing that displayed a large flak hole that was more air than metal.

> I will never forget when I heard that it was all over. I was in the Quonset hut sitting on my bunk. The squadron commander was walking by our quarters as we heard over the PA system the Japanese had surrendered.
>
> Without a thought I grabbed my .45 automatic and emptied it into the floor of the hut. The colonel was not impressed and I immediately received a stern "Sergeant, put that gun away!" to which I replied, "yes sir!" But, as soon as the words were out of my mouth all hell let lose around the camp with the sound of gunfire from pistols, rifles and machine guns all competing against each other in what sounded like the world's largest turkey shoot. Looking back, perhaps it was my gun going off that set the rest of the camp off! Everyone had been wound up so tight for so long it wasn't surprising that we all let off a little steam at the news.

Emperor Hirohito never talked of surrender or defeat in his speech, but accepting the terms of the Potsdam Declaration, he said, "the war situation has developed not necessarily to Japan's advantage, while the general trends of the world have all turned against her interest". An understatement if ever there was one; three million of his countrymen were dead.

He went on to say that the enemy had employed a new and most cruel bomb, which would result in an ultimate collapse and obliteration of the Japanese nation and would also lead to the total extinction of human civilization.

> Hirohito's speech was broadcast to the Japanese prisoners of war we had on Guam. They bowed their heads on hearing it and some were in tears. This was the first time that Hirohito had ever addressed his people; until that day his subjects had never heard his voice.

Such was the power of the A-bomb. Without it the war may have dragged on and ultimately necessitated an invasion of Japan by American forces.

The US feared that this ground war with Japan would result in massive military casualties. First and foremost, upon U.S. forces invading Japan, and secondly, as Japanese officers had been ordered to immediately kill every prisoner of war (POW), some 63,500 Allied captives, poor souls, would die.

Operation Downfall was the code name for the invasion of Japan. It was to be enacted in two phases. The first was called Operation Olympic and would have involved 250,000 army troops and more than 87,000 marines invading Kyushu, the southernmost of Japan's islands. The idea was to set up airbases there, so that air cover could be given to troops invading Tokyo Bay in the second phase. The problem was that in August 1945 there were already 370,000 Japanese ground troops and 575,000 home defense forces on Kyushu, and Operation Olympic was scheduled for November of that year. The Japanese had known for a long time that Kyushu was the logical site for an invasion and had begun preparing for such a situation as early as 1944. They could, by August 1945, accurately assess the strength of a US invasion and guess the locations they would target. US forces arriving on November 1, 1945 would have found a well-entrenched enemy. The US was prepared for a big fight and planned to send in huge numbers of war-ships; forty-two aircraft carriers, twenty-four battleships, almost four hundred destroyers and escorts. Even though American troops would outnumber the Japanese by three to one, it was going to be a tough fight. Chemical warfare was considered an option in the invasion as neither Japan nor the US were signatories to the Geneva Protocol which outlawed it. The Japanese had used chemical weapons against the Chinese in Manchuria, which opened the door for the US to use them should they see fit[10]. Given the circumstances there is little doubt that casualties would have been extremely high on both sides.

The second phase was Operation Coronet. Its objective was to invade Honshu at the Tokyo plain and was set to begin on December 1, 1945. Later it was postponed to March 1946. This would have been the largest amphibious operation in history. As the Japanese had committed so many resources to defending Kyushu they had little by way of defense against Operation Coronet. The British and their Commonwealth Allies were also to be involved with a naval force that included more than twelve aircraft

[10] www.en.wikipedia.org

carriers and several battleships. The operation would also have required considerable assistance from other allied forces from Europe, South Asia and Australia.[11]

There are various estimates of what the casualties might have been, but a figure of 250,000 is often talked of with 95,000 killed or injured in the first 90 days. Another article[12] states that the Joint Chiefs of Staff in April, 1945 produced a study that showed that there would be 7.45 Allied casualties per 1000 man-days and 1.78 fatalities per 1000 man-days. If we take these figures and apply them to Operation Olympic lasting 90-days, we can predict 456,000 casualties and 109,000 dead or missing in action for that operation alone. If we then add Operation Coronet, lasting another 90-days, the total number of casualties reaches 1.2 million and 267,000 deaths.

Other models were put forward at the time, including a study by General MacArthur's staff which estimated 23,000 casualties in the first 30-days and 125,000 after 120-days. This final figure was later reduced to 105,000. Similar figures came from other military advisers for Operation Olympic and cited 31,000 to 49,000 casualties in the first 30-days. Admiral Leahy estimated the total casualties at 268,000, or 35% of the invading Allied forces. Most of these estimates did not include losses at sea, and it has been said that they were based on intelligence that underestimated the number of Japanese soldiers and the effect suicide attackers would have on casualties and deaths.

Finally, a study carried out by William Shockley for Navy Secretary Henry Stimpson, came up with figures that exceeded most of the others. It put forward that there would be 1.7 to 4.0 million American casualties, an estimate that included 400,000 to 800,000 fatalities. A staggering five to ten million Japanese deaths were predicted. This assumed a large-scale involvement by Japanese civilians in the fighting.[13]

It was this potential for unprecedented loss of life that made President Truman decide to use the ultimate weapon on Japan. Critics have said that the casualty predictions were inflated to justify using the Atom bomb, but there is no doubt, given the willingness of the average Japanese person to

[11] Ibid
[12] Ibid
[13] Ibid

lay down his or her life for their country rather than surrender (even in the face of overwhelming odds), that casualties would have been very high. A further indication of the validity of these predictions is provided by the fact that 500,000 Purple Hearts[14] were made in anticipation of all the casualties and fatalities during Operation Olympic alone.

Japan's strategy in response to an invasion was simple; they would send a staggering two million troops to fight to their death, and rely on the fact that Japanese soldiers had more stomach for death and glory than their enemy, offering up what can only be termed - fanatical resistance.

While all this was going on Japanese aircraft engineers were building a secret Air Force. Back in the 1930's they had started to develop a range of modern war planes, but as the war started to look bad for them they stepped up this work. They moved their aircraft manufacturing into the mountains, burying it deep in caves, tunnels and mines, protecting it from the reach of the B-29's bombs.

Deep in the mountains Japanese designers worked on improving German airplane designs with the help of blueprints and plans from the Germans. These were no ordinary planes, they were technologically advanced, rocket and jet propelled models.

At the time the U.S. had no idea of the sheer numbers of aircraft being built, or the fact that they were so technologically advanced. Some 12,000 aircraft were being prepared to attack American ships and troops. One of these new 'super-aircraft' was specifically designed to attack B-29's. It was based on the Messerschmitt Me 163 Komet which was an amazingly fast, single seat, rocket propelled aircraft that could climb to over 9,000 meters in a little over two minutes and had the ability to glide for long periods waiting for its prey. It was armed with two 30mm canons and later versions carried 24 R4/M rockets which could down a bomber with one shot. The Japanese version was to be an improvement on even this highly advanced and deadly aircraft.

Fortunately, the war ended before these aircraft could be brought into service. If the war had dragged on and a land invasion taken place the cost

[14] The Purple Heart: A History of America's Oldest Military Decoration by Frederic Borch and F.C. Brown. The Last Great Victory: The End of World War II July-August 1945 by Sinney Weintraub

in American lives would have been extremely high and Herb's life would have got a whole lot more dangerous.

No one knows for sure what would have happened had Truman decided to continue with the daily bombing attacks on Japan and held off on dropping the bomb. Perhaps the B-29's would have eventually worn down Japan's resolve; what is certain however, is that dropping Little Boy and Fat Man hastened the end of the war and undoubtedly saved a considerable number of Allied lives.

Sixty years on, we can look back and gain a little perspective on Operation Downfall, and say with little fear of contradiction, that had it taken place it would have been a long and hard-fought battle during which hundreds of thousands of brave young Americans would have died on foreign soil. In the entire war we lost 300,000 people and suffered a little over one million casualties. Without the Atom bomb the numbers would have undoubtedly been far higher, quite possibly double this figure. When researching this subject it is not hard to discover extreme comments in the mass of documentation which has been created over the last sixty years, and inconsistencies abound. What seems to be fact is that the United States' military manpower policy in 1945 indicated that a loss of 100,000 casualties a month could be sustained from November 1945 through to the following fall, while remaining pretty much fully manned. This was to be achieved through the use of personnel reassigned from units that had been demobilized, and by using new Selective Service inductees. This illustrates that whatever the true estimates were at the time, the number of casualties expected by the administration was exceptionally high.

The debate as to whether it was morally right will carry on as long as there are people around to discuss it. As for Herb, it meant that his nearly daily trips to enemy territory were almost over. From his perspective they were the enemy; an enemy that would cut his head off if they caught him, just as they had with hundreds of his fellow airmen. To Herb, the means justified the end, the end of the war, the end of Japan as a military power.

So, as of August 15, the offensive against Japan ended, but it was not the end of the war for our brave B-29 crews; they still had a job to do, and many would still lose their lives over the next few weeks.

For the next few days the thundering engines of the B-29's are stilled on Guam. But then, on 27 August a new battle commences and the B-29's switch from dropping bombs to dropping food, medical supplies and clothing to American POWs. The first drop, to Weihsien Camp near Peking, China, is followed by 900 more in a matter of weeks. Four thousand, four hundred and seventy tons of supplies are dropped to approximately 63,500 prisoners in 154 camps. Seventy-seven crew members die in this effort and eight B-29's are lost. One more is attacked by Soviet fighters over North Korea. The war may be over, but as the rest of the world celebrates the end of the war to end all wars, the brave young men who fought it are still losing their lives.

15-30 August, 1945

In Guam, Herb and the crew of the City of Monroe were without an aircraft. She had battled through everything the enemy and the weather could throw at her for mission after mission, but 54 flak holes was more than even she could bear.

> She was special to us, a great aircraft, the best. We had flown 23 combat missions together and three training flights over Rota so we were very fond of the old girl. She had even flown at times without many of the controls you normally think essential, but now she was in the hands of aero repair, where she had to wait her turn. The overall control system needed to be checked and adjusted and then she needed to be test flown to ensure she had been repaired properly and was in tip-top working order.

> I tell you, we would all have given her blood had she needed it. That's how strongly we felt for her. She wasn't just a hunk of metal to us, she was one of the team and she had saved our lives on many occasions.

> Time crept by very slowly as we waited. On the one hand we were eager to get home, on the other we wanted our ship returned to us so we could get back into action. There's nothing worse than hanging around doing nothing. We became quite a nuisance to the mechanics working on the City of Monroe and would menace them regularly as we checked on her progress.

> When my brother Don was not flying we would meet up, 'acquire' a jeep, and go down to Tumon Bay. We'd last gone in late July and had a great time. We made a good team at getting our hands on a jeep as he was an officer and

I had a military driver's license. On this occasion we acted like kids playing on the beach collecting small seashells, coconuts and floating in the surf.

Herb's brother, Don remembers these trips and recalls that Herb had a knack for getting things done. *"We were at North Field on the northern tip of the island. One day we got the idea we would like to go visit the Navy on the south end, maybe get a beer from them and do some swimming. Transportation was scarce and we needed a jeep. I didn't have pull enough to get one, but Herb did. He knew the motor pool Sgt. and was able to acquire a jeep for the day. I was permitted to sign for the vehicle as my contribution since I was an officer".* He goes on to describe the day *"...anyway, we had a great time, even got Herb to climb trees on the beach to get us coconuts. On the way back to North Field at night, we had great fun. Huge jumping frogs would hop onto the muddy road and into our headlights. Our sport, was to run over them and hear the loud "pop" as they exploded".*

There were sure a lot of frogs on Guam and, unlike the Japs that were still loose on the island, the damn things always seemed to be on the main roads. When we went out in a jeep we would run them over all the time. I never did find out why they liked the road so much, maybe it was the heat radiating from it. They were certainly adventurous, risking their lives, and I bet we ran over six to ten of them every time we went out. They were large too, about the size of a saucer.

During this period I made good use of the dining hall as an attempt to make up for the meals missed while flying. Some played poker but I was determined to send all my money home. And then our lady was returned to us, as beautiful as ever, but unfortunately starting to show her age mechanically.

As soon as the City of Monroe was ready to fly again the crew was told they were to fly prisoner of war (POW) missions.

The 20 August, 1945 edition of Time magazine was simply a red sun with a black cross painted through it. The similarity to the 7 May, 1945 edition depicting Hitler with a red cross through his face was marked.

Now that it was all coming to an end I remember thinking back to my life as it was when I was 19. The world was simpler back then and consisted of my family, my job, and of course all the normal things a teenager gets in to. It wasn't until the war, and more specifically my relationship with the City of Monroe and its crew, and the missions we flew and endured, that I felt I truly gained a much broader and expanded concept of life, humanity, humility and the common struggle of all living beings.

My crew members and I all had a 'kill them before they kill us' attitude; it came with the job I think. We would continuously ask ourselves "why has this war happened now in the prime of our lives?" or more to the point "why us?" and "why did we return yesterday but others did not?" and then even deeper, philosophical questions like "why would a being greater than me, which I call my God, let such a thing happen to so many people," and "why were some born only to begin their lives and then have them snuffed out, while others go on to live long and healthy lives?"

I learned more in those few months of horror than I had in all my previous years on earth.

30 August, 1945

Mission #23 POW Supplies, SENDAI. Carried 9000 pounds of groceries swung in bomb bay for prisoners of war in Japan. The camp we dropped them in was 300 miles north of Tokyo, they were out in the yard waving to us. 18-hr mission, had to land at Iwo for fuel. Tired when we got back.

Sometimes Herb's diary entries epitomize the humility of the brave young man he truly was. He makes it sound like it was no big deal. You know, fly over to Japan, drop a few pallets of supplies and fly back. Well now, let's listen to Herb tell the story of this mission sixty years on, with some encouragement by the authors.

We recognized the camp easy enough, with it's POW flag flying on top. It looked like rows of ramshackle chicken houses – not like the sort of place humans should have to live in. There was a fence all around it, but the gates were hanging off their hinges.

The men would use anything to make sure the pilots could locate their camp. Some painted messages on the roofs, or laid out whitewashed stones; others flew national flags (US, British, French, Dutch), others just said POW. Some painted their unit details and the name of their aircraft or Bomb Group, while others, the number of prisoners in the camp.

This time we weren't carrying death and destruction; we had pallets of food, clothing, medicine, cigarettes, and according to Major Jones, some "Whitman's Samplers" and bottled beer.

We made a couple of passes over the camp to judge the wind. We wanted to make sure the parachutes drifted down in a suitable spot and not injure any of our boys on the ground.

Herb's crew were obviously being careful because there had been a few close calls as other aircraft had dropped pallets of supplies which crashed through the roofs of barracks. Bob Goldsworthy, a POW in the Omori camp, tells of one drop that didn't go entirely to plan[15]. A case of soap crashed through the roof of his barracks, missing him by only a few feet. He remembers that it was Cashmere Bouquet Soap. It is interesting to note that this brand is still available today. He comments, *"I thought, what a hell of a thing, to live through prison life only to get killed by a case of soap. But the food that was dropped saved lives."*

In fact, two prisoners were killed when a supply barrel crashed through the roof of their barracks. The prisoners subsequently laid out white rocks in a field within the stockade that spelled out "DO NOT DROP HERE. TWO MEN KILLED."[16]

We reduced our altitude to 500 to 600 feet and dropped the lifesaving supplies next to a hillside right across from the camp. The pallets, stacked with canvas bags, each had a parachute attached with ripcords tied to a line and a cable. These were in turn attached to the inside of the aircraft so when the pallets were dropped, the ripcords tripped the parachute and hopefully, it opened.

There were tools attached to the pallets to help the men open these veritable feasts.

It is interesting to note here that by the time the crew of the City of Monroe were airborne again, hundreds of supply drops had already been made. At the beginning, these drops didn't always go as planned. At one point it is reported that 47% of the parachutes failed to open.

[15] A conversation held online between Jack Blevins a B-29 crew member and Bob Goldsworthy on the 56 Years Today site
http://home.att.net/~sallyann6/b29/56years-4508b.html.
[16] http://home.att.net/~sallyann6/b29/56years-4508b.html

This prompted crews to drop outside of the prison compounds rather than take a risk by getting the supplies too close. Mostly, the B-29 crews did an amazing job of dropping the supplies close to the prisoners without mishap.

Some crews reported that locals were seen taking the supplies to the camps for the prisoners. POW camps usually housed between 100 and 200 men.

> All our load fell as planned and it was heartwarming to see our boys come running out to fetch the supplies. They crossed a stream so fast and in such large numbers that we could see the splashes rising out of the water. By my estimation there was about 200 of them, all looking very thin, but if there was anything seriously wrong with them they sure as heck forgot about it long enough to get those supplies. They reached the hillside where everything had landed and we could see them tearing the wrapping off and waving hello and thank-you. It felt real good to be able to do this for them after all they had suffered. The frightening thing was that they were the lucky ones; so many had been executed by the Japs.

Herb's feeling of euphoria at making a successful drop didn't last long. The ripcords from the parachute drop were dangling out of the bomb bay preventing the doors from latching and remaining closed. This was a lot more serious than it sounds. If the doors weren't properly latched they would continue to pop back open. With the bomb bay doors open the City of Monroe would not make it safely back to Iwo Jima; the drag on the aircraft would use up additional fuel and they would very likely be forced to ditch in open ocean.

> I took my pocketknife out and went out into the front bomb bay while Tommy, the ring gunner, went to the rear bomb bay. We worked our way around the bomb racks and reached out over the open bomb bay and began cutting the cords. Approximately sixteen cords had to be cut and it took a long time, as they were very thick and made of strong nylon.

At this point Herb is working in the open bomb bay with the wind whipping around him and he has no parachute. The space they are working in is very small and could not be accessed while wearing a parachute. Herb and Tommy are risking their lives to save the ship, and prevent a date with the cold Pacific.

We had to hold on to the bomb rack with our right arm and cut with our left hand. We had to cut away all the cords or the door wouldn't close and latch, it was time consuming, tiring and pretty scary. Everything was bouncing around and it was cold and we were at the mercy of the wind. I'd made it through 23 combat missions and didn't want to fall out of the aircraft on a supply drop, especially without a parachute.

Eventually they managed to clear the bomb bay doors and get safely back into the aircraft. With the doors closed and latched they could safely return to Iwo. Once back on Iwo Jima, Herb was grateful to be back on solid ground. He comments, sixty years later:

I had exhausted all my adrenaline during this unusual mission and was ready to collapse. Later I commented that any future involvement in aeronautical acrobatics would consist of me being a spectator standing firmly on the surface of the earth and looking skyward.

That is an understatement, if ever there was one. Most of us could not imagine risking life and limb hanging out of an aircraft trying to get the bomb bay doors closed. This is the stuff of James Bond movies, not real life. But, to Herb it was just an 'unusual mission.'

A few days later, on 4, September, the whole crew of a B-29 was lost flying a POW mission in the southern Sendai region.

DISPLAY OF
FORCE
(SEPTEMBER 1945)

CHAPTER TEN

*Proclaim liberty throughout all the land unto
all the inhabitants thereof.*

–inscription on the Liberty Bell

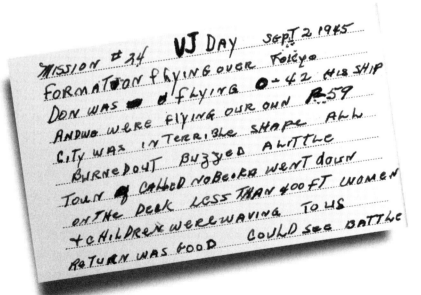

MISSION #24   VJ DAY   SEPT 2 1945
FORMATION FLYING OVER TOKYO
DON WAS FLYING 0-42 HIS SHIP
AND WE WERE FLYING OUR OWN B-59
CITY WAS IN TERRIBLE SHAPE ALL
BURNED OUT BUZZED A LITTLE
TOWN CALLED NOBEOKA WENT DOWN
ON THE DECK LESS THAN 400 FT WOMEN
& CHILDREN WERE WAVING TO US
RETURN WAS GOOD   COULD SEE BATTLE

NEWS

September sees the end of WWII with General Douglas MacArthur and Admiral Chester Nimitz accepting the final and official surrender of Japan aboard the battleship Missouri in Tokyo Bay, from a delegation led by Mamoru Shigemitsu.

IvaToguri D'Aquino, a Japanese-American suspected of being wartime radio propagandist "Tokyo Rose," is arrested in Yokohama. Japanese Prime Minister Hideki Tojo tries to commit suicide to avoid facing a war crimes tribunal.

Japanese troops surrender in various locations across the Pacific where they have been holding out and the Japanese army formally surrenders in Singapore.

Back in the U.S. the movie 'Orders From Tokyo' documents the wartime atrocities of the Japanese in Manila; for the masses John Garfield and Eleanor Parker star in a gritty war story 'Pride of the Marines' that tells the story of an embittered marine who was blinded by a grenade and whose girlfriend eventually helps him realize that his sacrifice was worthwhile; on a lighter note Walt Disney reissued Pinocchio – interestingly in 1945 it was already a classic.

2 September, 1945

Emperor Hirihito signs the official instrument of surrender onboard the USS Missouri in Tokyo Bay.

For Herb, this is a very special day; he is flying in a massive formation of 500 B-29's, ahead of 450 carrier aircraft from the 3rd Fleet, over the USS Missouri, in a show of force that would not be forgotten and was unlike anything anyone had ever experienced.

> "2 September, 1945, Mission #24. VJ Day, Formation flying over Tokyo. Don (my brother) was flying 0-42, his ship, and we were flying our own P-59. City was in terrible shape, all burned out. Buzzed a little town called Nobeoko, went down on the deck to less than 400 feet; women & children were waving to us."

> "Return was good and we could see battleship Missouri out in Tokyo Bay."

It was quite a day, the noise alone was deafening. One B-29 is quite a noisy beast, but get 500 at once flying at low altitudes, in formation, and you have a sound that reverberates across the countryside. If there were any civilians questioning Japan's decision to surrender this would certainly answer them. As Earl Johnson reports on the '56 Years Ago' website,[17] formation was a term that could only be used loosely; getting twelve aircraft together is tough enough, but several hundred! The B-29's assembled far to the north of the Missouri and then headed south for Tokyo Bay at set times. Once they passed over the ship they turned east, went back to northern Japan and turned back south to make a second pass. It all took an hour or so. To those on the ground it must have been quite awe-inspiring to see so many aircraft in one place at one time for such a continuously long period. Of course looking up they would not have realized that they were seeing the same aircraft twice.

> After we had made our two passes over the city we decided to drop down and take a closer look. I left my station and went up front to have a look at the devastation. We flew above a small town at about 400 feet and the women and children were waving at us. It felt strange to be welcomed by these people who had suffered an unremitting battering over the last several months. I guess they were glad the war was over.

> We were usually here at night, bombing under cover of darkness, so this was the first time I had had a chance to see the level of destruction we had brought to Tokyo. The city was nothing but burned ash and charcoal; all the buildings had been gutted.

> I am sure I speak for the whole crew of the City of Monroe when I say we did not want to kill people, but believed that not only were our lives in jeopardy but those of our families and fellow Americans back home. We were fighting to protect the freedom of our country and for its very existence.

> We were not focused on killing the enemy, but accomplishing the job at hand and saving the lives and freedoms of the American people. I am not sure we could have achieved what we did in any other way.

Herb talks of buzzing the outskirts of Tokyo as if it was a normal thing to do. In fact quite a number of B-29's went down for a closer look, but this

---

[17] http://home.att.net/~sallyann6/b29/56years-4509a.html

CHAPTER TEN

sightseeing was totally against orders. Some even buzzed the Missouri. General MacArthur was not impressed and was extremely angry at the 20th Air Force and especially the B-29 pilots for poor military discipline, even more so as some of the B-29's did not carry out the second pass before breaking out of formation.

Of course, the boys had gone through a lot so it was understandable that they felt the urge to cut loose and see what Japan looked like after millions of pounds of incendiaries and high explosives had been dropped on it.

30 September, 1945

September 30, 1945. Force display mission. Ship #O 41 over Korea.

Takeoff: 0230 AM, Sunday morning. Aircraft Commander Lt J. T. Cox, Co-pilot Lt D. E. Greer (brother Don). Trip was a force display over Korea to impress the Koreans that we could get bombers there to bomb them in case of any trouble they started.

We took off from Guam and flew to Iwo Jima, over Iwo we turned left for Kyushu. We crossed Iwo at sunrise. We crossed the northern tip off Kyushu to a little Island by the name of Tsushima where our assembly point was; after we formed into formation, (10 ships) we flew to Pusan, Korea, from there on a course taking us through Taegu, Kumchow, Kumsan, Kanggyong and down to Kunsan on the coast where we could look out over the Yellow Sea.

Our return from Kunsan took us through Choin, Namwon, Sunchow, Yosuand out into the bay where we broke up formation and headed for Iwo. We had to follow another ship because our Loran, compass, and radar were out.

We hit Iwo Jima about 03:30 - 04:00 in the afternoon where we went on a heading of 165 degrees to Guam. We arrived at Guam about 08:30 after passing through quite a bit of bad weather.

I helped Don (my brother) fly all the way from Kyushu to about 200 miles from Guam. He was in the right seat and I was in the left. Trip was very good. 18 hrs flying time covered over 3,500 statute miles. We carried 2 bomb bay tanks and 200 rounds of ammo per gun loaded hot.

186| FIRE FROM THE SKY: A DIARY OVER JAPAN

Don had been on Guam since mid-July although I didn't know he was there for a while. He was a co-pilot of a B-29 flying out of the same airfield. We probably even flew on some of the same missions together.

I used to check on how he was doing once in a while, but we had our work to do and of course both of us kept with our crew a lot.

The 'Force Display' mission over Korea was meant as a warning that the United States Army Air Corps was quite capable of entering their territory, flying out of Guam, Tinian and other bases, with as many B-29's as it wanted.

When I heard that Don was scheduled to take part in the display of force I decided to see if I could somehow go with him. I asked Major Jones whether he would give me authorization to go along as a passenger in my brother's plane. He was really understanding and approved my absence.

I flew the mission sitting between the Aircraft Commander Lt. J.T. Cox and my brother who was the co-pilot. We flew and maintained an altitude of 10,000 feet in order that we could easily be seen by the people on the ground. On the way back I was allowed to take control of the plane and for the first time, my dream of being a pilot came true, if only for a short period of time.

Moving On

CHAPTER ELEVEN

Flying with my brother had been a great experience and I was already thinking about how we might arrange it again in the not too distant future.

Major Luther A. Jones, my Aircraft Commander and pilot of the City of Monroe said that I was the "best damn radio operator in the South Pacific" – this was quite a compliment and I thanked him for it. On my part I felt fortunate that I had been lucky enough, right from the outset, to have a pilot who had flown some two thousand hours in a B-29, not to mention that he had been a trainer for combat crews at bombing, radio and navigation schools. I could easily have been attached to a crew with a pilot that only had a few hundred hours on these huge behemoths.

Jones managed to pull us through the war safely, with only a few bumps and scrapes to show for the dozens of missions and close calls we had experienced. He was certainly my choice for best pilot and I think I can speak for the rest of the crew when I say we wouldn't have wanted anyone else.

During the battle for Iwo Jima, Admiral Chester W. Nimitz was quoted as saying; "Among the Americans who served on Iwo Island, uncommon valor was a common virtue." This could easily be said of all the men who participated in the WWII efforts against Japan, and for those who were privileged to fly B-29's, their "Cadillacs" in the sky, uncommon valor was indeed a common daily occurrence.

The young men, really boys, who fought this war, did not mature in any normal way. Instead of gradually learning and understanding responsibility and accountability for themselves and their actions, they were thrown into a situation where they had the responsibility, not only for their own lives, but for the lives of their families, friends and the American way of life resting squarely on their shoulders – a heavy burden to carry while being scared to death. Herb says it best.

> We were, in essence, robbed of our youth – our boyish times – by a thief in the night, a black specter, or should I say red? I believe this fast evolution from boy to hardened man caused problems later in our emotional make-up. It certainly affected the way we observed life and the way we reacted to it.

If we are to learn anything from WWII it is that man's inhumanity to man knows no boundaries. The atomic bomb may have brought about the end of Herb's war, but it did not prevent further wars breaking out in every corner of the world. The men and women in our armed forces are still dying on foreign soil, still giving their lives for their country. As Herb found out during the spring and summer of 1945, freedom isn't free and now sixty years on he still relives the horror of firebombing Japan.

Post-war, surplus B-29's were refitted and modified for, scientific experiments, testing and other non-war advancements, but by the mid-60s only a few remained. The B-29 was in fact, a pioneer in the development of in-flight refueling systems and used in one-way missions at the start of the Cold War when some 18 B-29's were sent to the United Kingdom. Also, a significant number of aircraft built since the War were based upon the brilliant design of this amazing airplane.

In the early 1970's, a team of Confederate Air Force (CAF) Colonels (later renamed Commemorative Air Force) selected a B-29 from the few remaining at the Navy Weapons Center in China Lake, California, and began the long and expensive process of restoring it to flying condition. Col. Victor

N. Agather had been on the wartime development team for the aircraft, and agreed to sponsor the acquisition and restoration. On August 2, 1971, the B-29 became airborne for the first time in 17 years and arrived safely, six hours later, at Harlingen, Texas. In honor of Col. Agather's contributions and dedication to the B-29 project, the aircraft was named Fifi, after Mrs. Agather. For more than twenty years, Fifi has been the only B-29 still regularly flying, visiting memorials and airshows across the country.

As the writing of this book was in its final stages, Ron and Herb Greer successfully promoted their bid to host Fifi in their hometown during the 50th Anniversary and "Air Show" celebration at Little Rock Air Force base in early October 2005. After all these years Herb will have an opportunity to reacquaint himself with one of the world's greatest aircraft ever; perhaps not his beloved City of Monroe, but one of her sisters. This time when he steps aboard the Superfortress it will be in celebration of the 60th anniversary of the end of the Pacific war rather than to fly into danger and mayhem.

It was Fifi that brought Luther Jones and Herbert Greer back together after 57 years on Veterans Day 2002. The two comrades met once again, after more than five decades, in Monroe, Louisiana to honor the aircraft that had been such an important part of their young lives.

Luther passed away February 26, 2005 but in the three years since their reunion Luther and Herb were able to spend much quality time together telling stories, and on occasion stretching the truth. It is ironic that it was the worlds' only flying B-29 Fifi that brought these two crewmembers back together. The Aviation & Military Museum of Louisiana has recently donated a refurbished radio system to Fifi in honor of Maj. Luther Jones, aircraft commander, and S/Sgt. Herbert L. Greer, radio operator, of the B-29 City of Monroe.

But, what happened to the City of Monroe, you may ask? She returned to the United States on 21 May, 1946 and was put into storage at Ogden Air Materiel Center, Hill AFB UT. She was in service for less than a year and subsequently remained in storage until 1 January 1951 when she was scrapped. An ignominious end to a great aircraft, only made worse by the fact that the record card of her existence states that her name was City of Onroe[18].

[18] Archie DiFante, Archivist, Archives Branch, AFHRA/RSA600, Chennault Circle, Maxwell AFB AL 36112-6424 USA. Tel: (334) 953-2447

During the four years it took to research and write this book more than a million[19] veterans of World War II have passed away (1,056 a day according to a Department of Veterans Affairs estimation). Who will speak for these individuals as well as those 'true heroes' who never returned to their families and loved ones? Those that died during the war who had their lives snuffed out like candles on a birthday cake, but without the ceremony? These young men would not have had too many candles on their cakes when celebrating their last birthdays; they were young and were experiencing the feeling of immortality that comes with youth. For many that feeling was the ultimate lie. They knew what was expected of them, why they were needed and were ready to do whatever it took, including losing their lives, to ensure the continued freedom of their fellow countrymen.

WWII is already being forgotten. One day, quite soon, there will be no one left to tell our children what it was really like. No eyewitness accounts. Fewer and fewer schools teach it, or if they do, their interpretation lacks the gut-wrenching reality of what really happened. The history of WWII is not only about facts and dates; it is about the men who lost their lives and about those whose lives were changed forever.

While our war heroes are still with us we need to get their stories down on paper or recorded any way we can. The story of Staff Sergeant Herbert L. Greer is one story among many. Just one perspective of a moment in time, immortalized by a fading memory in a vibrant spirit.

Lest we forget – freedom is not free.

[19] http://www.cnn.com/2004/US/05/29/war.memorial/

POSTSCRIPT

Luther A. Jones died February 26, 2005 at the age of 87. He flew tens of thousands of miles in the aircraft he named and saved the lives of his crew on more than one occasion. He was a great pilot and a great man. He will be sorely missed not only by Herb, but also by the country he fought for.

During Herb's flying days as a radio operator he managed to save some 32 airmen by contacting Air Sea Rescue on three separate occasions. On 29 May 1945 the crew of Slic Chic was shot down between Japan and Iwo Jima and 7 of the 11 crewmembers were rescued. In 1948 a B-29 had ditched off of Okinawa and a Air Rescue Flying Boat with a crew of 3 attempting a rescue took on water and broke into pieces. Herb managed to contact a Naval vessel that was able to pick up the 11 member crew and 3 man crew. Again in 1948, during a typhoon, a B-29 crew of 11 ditched on Fais Island in the Ulithis group and Herb picked up the Gibson Girl SOS and alerted Air Rescue for pick up.

Once Herb's brother Don enlisted in 1943, the two brothers attempted to fly together but discovered it was not possible. The military had a policy against it after five brothers from the Sullivan family of Waterloo, Iowa were killed in action when their ship, the USS Juno, was torpedoed at Guadalcanal the previous year.

Typical of Herb though, and a tribute to his wily ways, was that they still managed to fly together a few times towards the end of the war. It wasn't until the Korean War however, that they managed to make it more permanent.

In 1949 Herb was in Spokane, Washington working as a radio instructor and Don, recently back in the Air Force after finishing college, was to be stationed in Alaska, just at the time things were heating up in Korea. It was at this time the Air Force was asking for volunteers to fly combat missions over Korea. Don approached his commanding officer and said that he would volunteer on condition he could fly with his brother.

Unexpectedly the C.O. looked kindly on this unusual request and in spite of some reluctance from the Air Force, the brother's parents were asked whether they would agree to their sons flying together. They gave their blessing and, with the confidence of their family ringing in their ears, Herb and Don were on their way back to Japan. This was July 1950.

Herb and Don found security in knowing that they were watching after each other. As Herb says, "In a tight situation you want to know you can rely on the other person one hundred percent"

Don tells the story of Herb piling sections of old flak jackets under his seat on their second mission. On their first mission, they had encountered heavy flak and Herb wanted to make sure his brother was as safe as possible.

They had a strong feeling of security fighting this war together and it paid off. Unbelievably, after flying 36 missions between them during the Pacific War, they flew a further 31 missions together over Korea in their beloved B-29's, with Herb as radio operator and Don as pilot.

No one is absolutely certain, but it is thought that they are the only brothers that flew combat missions together in two wars. They left combat duty in Korea, November 1950.

Don continued his career in the Air Force, learning to fly jet bombers and later in his career, to arm nuclear bombs. He was serving as Military Aide to Eugene M. Zuckert, Secretary of the Air Force when he retired. He had previously been Executive Officer to Dr. Joseph Charyk, Under Secretary of the Air Force for Research & Development. Don retired at the urging of Dr. Charyk to help him start COMSAT Corporation. He was in that position at the time President Kennedy was assassinated and was part of the team on Air Force Two that brought everyone home from Dallas.

Herb went on to serve in B-36's, B-47's and B-52's, fuelling his love of flying, ignited so many years before by a wooden biplane landing in a farmer's field. During his military career Herb accummulated some 14,000 hours of flight time. If we compare this to a non-military work week of 40 hours at 52 weeks in a year this equals 2,080 hours. With Herb's 14,000 hours equated to 2,080 hours per year we see that Herb would have spent almost 7 years working off the ground and in the '*wild blue yonder*'.

He retired at Little Rock Air Force base and lives to this day, with his son Ron, just a few miles from the base.

It would be remiss of us to close this tale of honor without mentioning that on 5 May, 2001, Herb and Don, received the Republic of Korea War Service Medal, from Major General Nels Running, Director of the 50th anniversary Korean War commemoration and the Korean Ambassador to the United States. Their 98-year old mother, Nellie Greer, received certificates of appreciation from the California State Legislature, the California State Senate and the Department of Defense, signed by Secretary Donald Rumsfeld, for her contribution in allowing her sons to fly together.

A fitting end to a story of self-sacrifice, bravery and a commitment to fight for freedom.

References/
Sources

Mission Chronologies

The three primary resources for mission chronology and data were:

http://home.att.net/~sallyann6/b29/56years-4505b.html
56 Years Ago - This site was used extensively with the permission of
SallyAnn

http://39th.org/39th/history/chronology.htm
#39th Bomb Group History

http://www.usaaf.net/
United States Army Air Forces in World War II

Other information regarding missions was obtained from:

http://www.angelfire.com/in/rwachs/
20th Air Force - B-29 World War II Missions - Crew 31

http://www.usaaf.net/chron/45/may45.htm
United States Army Air Forces in World War II - Combat Chronology of
the US Army Air Forces May 1945

General Research

The Last Mission: Jim Smith
Publisher: Broadway (May 6, 2003) Paperback: ISBN: 0767907795

Flyboys: James Bradley
Publisher: Back Bay Books (September 14, 2004) Paperback: ISBN:
0316159433

The Blockbuster – Sunday June 10, 1945

Times-Pacayune (Newspaper) http://www.timespicayune.com/

http://www.questia.com/Index.jsp
Questia - The World's Largest Online Library

http://www.bbc.co.uk/history/war/wwtwo/japan_no_surrender_01.shtml
BBC UK

http://www.time.com/time/magazine/archive/coversearch?&year=1945
Time Magazine

http://edition.cnn.com/2004/US/05/29/war.memorial/
CNN International.com

http://acacia.pair.com/Acacia.Vignettes/Steele.B29.Bomber.html
Sergeant Steele and the B29 Bomber

By Judith Bronte
http://www.marketrends.net/WWIIsecret/mission.html
An Anthology of the Crew and a WWII B-29 Bomber, named "For The
Luvva Mike"

http://40thbombgroup.org/memories.html
AN ARCHIVE OF ISSUES OF 'MEMORIES'
(as published by the 40th Bomb Group Association)

http://www.ishipress.com/alden.htm
My Uncle was a Bomber Pilot over Japan in World War II

http://www.childrenofthemanhattanproject.org/ CG/CG_09C2.htm
509th Composite Group - The Historic Timelines

http://www.erieveterans.com/WW_II_Stories/Gaber___Karl/gaber___
karl.html
Karl Gaber - By BILL WELCH - Interviewed in May 1999

http://capefearww2.uncwil.edu/voices/pritchett103.html
University of North Carolina Wilmington Library - Interview with Mr.
Paul O'Neil Pritchett - A program which video tapes World War II veterans

http://www.historynet.com/wwii/
The History Net.com

http://www.ww2pacific.com/
World War II in the Pacific - Menu to The Early Years

http://www.worldwariihistory.info/
World War II History Reference Library

http://www.worldwar-2.net/timelines/asia-and-the-pacific/pacific-islands/pacific-islands-World War 2.net

http://www.au.af.mil/au/afhra/
Air Force Historical Research Agency - Maxwell AFB, Alabama

http://www.swaviator.com/html/issueAM00/eaglerockAM00.html
SW Aviator Online Edition - Alexander Eaglerock Biplane

http://www.csi.ad.jp/ABOMB/data.html
Introduction: About the A-Bomb

B-29 Sites

http://www.hill.af.mil/museum/photos/wwii/b-29.htm
Hill Aerospace Museum

http://www.ww2guide.com/b29ops.shtml
World War II Air Power -Boeing B-29 Superfortress (Model 345) VH Bomber

http://www.rootsweb.com/~ny330bg/aircraft.htm
The aircraft of the 330th BG

http://www.constable.ca/b29.htm
Boeing B-29 "Superfortress" Heavy Bomber

http://www.milehighcaf.org/b29.asp
Mile High Wing Commemorative Air Force

http://www.fiddlersgreen.net/AC/aircraft/Boeing-B29/info/info.htm
Boeing B-29 Superfortress Information

http://www.csd.uwo.ca/~pettypi/elevon/baugher_us/b029i.html
Boeing B-29 Superfortress

http://www.boeing.com/history/boeing/b29.html
Boeing Corporation

http://www.wpafb.af.mil/museum/air_power/ap20.htm
BOEING B-29 "SUPERFORTRESS

REFERENCES/SOURCES

Training Bases

http://www.globalsecurity.org/wmd/facility/amarillo.htm
Global Security.org - Amarillo AFB, TX

http://www.strategic-air-command.com/bases/Amarillo_AFB.htm
SAC Bases: Amarillo Air Force Base

http://www.airforcebase.net/usaf/joeslist.html
Joe McCusker's list of Air Force Bases

http://bellevilleillinois.homestead.com/scottairforcebase4.html
Scott Field

http://www.ctaz.com/~mocohist/museum/kaaf.htm
Mohave Museum of History and Arts - KINGMAN ARMY AIR FIELD

http://www.384thbg.iwarp.com/rs_lewisca1.htm
384th Bombardment Group

http://www.guideall.com/usafb.htm
Guide All - List of Air Bases

http://www.militarymuseum.org/AFPosts.html
The California Military Museum - Major Army Air Forces Installations
During World War II

http://www.geocities.com/alwood.geo/life.html
Life on the Base at North Field, Guam 1945 With the 314th BW(VH)

http://www.cargodog.net/b29/
Northwest Field, Guam, circa 1945

Armaments

http://www.ww2guide.com/bombs.shtml
World War II Air Power - Bombs Weapons Rockets Aircraft Ordnance

http://www.geocities.com/lastdingo/aviation/usbombs.htm
U.S. Bomb Types

http://www2.hawaii.edu/~dfukushi/Hotaru.html
Hotaru no Haka (Grave of the Fireflies)

http://users.erols.com/mwhite28/battles.htm#Auschwitz
Death Tolls for the Man-made Megadeaths of the 20th Century

ADVANCE PRAISE

"No man, who has not been there, knows the intensity of human emotions and the power of adrenaline that combat can release from the inner self. 'A Diary Over Japan' is an enlightening revelation of a young man-boy's experience documented in his personal diary.

As the radio operator on the B-29 Superfortress 'City of Monroe', Staff Sergeant Herb Greer would, in 24 long and grueling combat missions, explore the full spectrum of human emotions. From the initial jitters of expectation facing the unknown, to stark terror as the world around him exploded in brutal violence that is the heartbeat of combat, to professional satisfaction in completing the mission successfully, Herb would feel it all.

America sends its young sons and daughters to confront evil, fight for freedom of the oppressed and to preserve our freedom. Herb Greer and his brother, Don, served the cause of freedom in WWII and in Korea. I met these two warriors in Anderson, California in May of 2001, where they received the Korean War Service Medal from the Ambassador of the Republic of Korea. But these dutiful sons of 98-year-old Nellie Greer humbly deferred center stage to their mother as she received certificates of appreciation from California and from the Department of Defense for having petitioned the Air Force to let her two sons fly together in the B-29 during the Korean War. The Greer brothers flew 31 missions in Korea.

History is so often a cold recounting of facts and figures on a national or international scale. 'A Diary Over Japan' brings history to life at the personal level. This is a great read!"

Nels Running, Major General, USAF (Ret)
Executive Director of America's
Commemoration of the Korean War 2000 - 2003

"This book is one of the best researched books I have had the pleasure of reading. Thanks to Sgt. Greer, the crew of the "City of Monroe" and aircraft commander Maj. Jones who will be long remembered."

Rosemary Chennault Semicell, daughter of Gen. Claire Chennault and President, Aviation & Military Museum of Louisiana, Monroe.

"Herb Greer's daily diary accounting of the B-29 raids over Japan provides a vivid first-hand picture of how it was. This is a great read."

Lt. Colonel Donald E (Buzz) Wagner, USAF Ret'd.

"I salute you Herb and Ron Greer for your contribution to Pacific W.W.II History—FIRE FROM THE SKY! I was a member of that B-29 team and you've rewound History to that special place where your Dad and I served. Liberty and Freedom were on the line and after a very slow start out of the gate, we honored the call and persevered. Patrick Henry said, "I know of no way to judge the future, but by its past." Herein is an outstanding work that gives you the true heartbeat of that unprecedented time in our history where young God and Country Americans preserved Freedom and Liberty that was dangerously tested by world Dictatorship!"

Jim B. Smith B-29 Radio Operator of The Boomerang stationed at Northwest Field, Guam—author of The Last Mission!

"The more I read the more I believe Fire From The Sky should be required in all academia! Great going you guys! Nothing beats that diary venue. You are there. It's fresh and not covered or exaggerated by the pruning knife of time. Jim."

Jim B. Smith B-29 Radio Operator of The Boomerang stationed at Northwest Field, Guam--author of The Last Mission!